K8xxX4.15

S0-AUP-019

THE
SENTENCE

THE SENTENCE

PAULINE SMOLIN

University of Cincinnati

PHILIP T. CLAYTON

University of Cincinnati

D.C. HEATH AND COMPANY
Lexington, Massachusetts Toronto

Copyright © 1977 by D. C. Heath and Company.

All rights reserved. No part of this publication may be reproduced or transmitted in any form or by any means, electronic or mechanical, including photocopy, record-ing, or any information storage or retrieval system, without permission in writing from the publisher.

Published simultaneously in Canada.

Printed in the United States of America.

International Standard Book Number: 0-669-00783-8

Dear Student:

We are glad you are going to use this book because it will help you gain skill in understanding and writing correct sentences. This book was put together over a period of four years for and with our students, who, like you, for one reason or another, had not yet fully mastered the essentials of sentence structure. We learned from our students through trial and error how to help them learn what they needed to know about sentences, and we assure you that this book works. When you have finished working it through, you will be able to write correct sentences whenever you feel like it—or need to.

Before you start working, we would like to explain two principles this book is based on. The most important principle is that each of you is unique: each of you comes to this work with a different amount and kind of prior knowledge about sentences and each of you has your own pace of learning. The very idea of a workbook like this, which has each person work alone, is based on the recognition that different people learn at different rates and that the same person will grasp some skills very quickly but will grasp other skills only slowly. So remember, if you do your work carefully, when you finish this book, you will know all that you need to know about sentence structure.

Another important principle of this workbook is that learning is an active process, based on doing. In this process you, the learner, are the chief doer. In practical terms, this means that you will find yourself doing quite a lot of work. Our method in this book has been to break down each large skill into smaller parts (or concepts) and then to proceed as follows: (1) introduce you to each concept in the clearest words we can find, (2) give examples to help you understand the concept, and (3) ask you to put the concept into practice in increasingly difficult skill-building exercises. Thus, as you advance, you will be moving from simpler to more complicated skills, and your ability to perform the more complicated skills will depend on your understanding the simpler skills. Therefore, be sure you totally understand at each step along the way. If anything is unclear to you, be sure to ask for further explanation from those working with you. Remember that you are the important person here and that this workbook and the people you work with, teachers and tutors, have only one purpose—to help you learn.

One final point before you begin. This book has four sections; in all but the first section you can expect to get correct answers to nearly every exercise question. If you should make even one error, remember that it is extremely important that you correct it and master the concept involved before going on. But *Section One* is different. It introduces all the key terms about sentences that you need to know. As a result, this section probably will be difficult for you when you are first starting out. But don't worry too much if you have some problems with *Section One*. The other three sections will clarify all the key terms that *Section One* introduces.

We wish you good work, and now begin.

Sincerely,

Pauline Smolin

Philip Clayton

Some Recommendations to Teachers and Tutors For Use of This Book

1. This workbook contains many exercises to help the student understand and write correct sentences. Some of these exercises the student can check with the anwer key at the back of the book. Other exercises the teacher or tutor will check. Careful explanation about how you want the student to use this workbook will be most helpful in insuring the success of the student's work. If the student is to do the work at home instead of in a class or a writing lab, we recommend that the student not do more than a couple of exercises before bringing them in to be checked. This method will insure that any learning problem will be caught before it begins to interfere with the student's progress in understanding and writing correct sentences.

2. *Section One*, Sentence Fundamentals, is difficult since it introduces *all* the key terms about sentence structure. If students have difficulty with the exercises in *Section One*, do not let them get bogged down there. Explain that all these matters will be broken down in detail in the other sections of the book. *Section One*, along with the Writing Sample at the beginning of the book, should provide you with information about how much your students already know about sentence structure.

3. If students make more than two or three errors on Exercise Three (subject/verb recognition) in *Section One*, Sentence Fundamentals, they should go directly to *Section Two*, Verb Recognition, and do the entire section. They should then return to *Section One* and complete it before

going on to *Section Three*, <u>Sentence Elements</u>. If students have no problem with Exercise Three, they can finish *Section One*, skip *Section Two*, and go on to *Section Three*. (The instructions for this procedure are printed in the appropriate places.)

4. *Section Two*, <u>Verb Recognition</u>, is designed to teach the skill of recognizing words that function as verbs in sentences: its purpose is not to teach students to produce standard American English verb forms. We discourage dealing with problems of *s/es* and *d/ed* endings, subject-verb agreement, and irregular verbs at this point. Such problems are quite likely to come up in the exercises students do in this section. We recommend that you use these exercises as a diagnostic tool that may reveal the students' need to work on verb forms at a subsequent time, but not when they are trying to master sentence structure. Sentence structure has enough complexities without adding on all the complexities of the English verb system. We strongly believe that these two matters should be dealt with separately, putting sentence structure first and verb forms after.

A Note on Terminology

We have used the grammatical terms that we believe are most familiar to students, teachers, and tutors. And we have tried to stay with a minimum number of terms. Although much of what we have done in this book indirectly reflects linquistic studies of recent years, we have not used the special terminology of linguistics.

Acknowledgments

We wish to thank the students, tutors, and teachers whose responses and suggestions have helped us throughout the years of putting this book together. Special thanks to Dr. Stuart Blersch for volunteering to do the answer key.

Contents

Write a paragraph about one of the following topics that had an important effect on your life: an event, a person, a place, an object.

Your paragraph should have:
1. A sentence at the beginning giving your controlling idea.
2. At least six sentences that develop your idea.
3. A concluding sentence.

....

....

....

....

....

....

....

....

....

....

....

....

....

....

....

....

....

....

....

....

....

....

....

....

....

Show your paragraph to your instructor.

THE
SENTENCE

SECTION ONE

Sentence Fundamentals

The purpose of this section is to let you know from the start what this whole book will cover. Therefore this section briefly introduces all the key terms and concepts about sentences.

The sentence is the basic unit of thinking, speaking, and writing. In writing, a sentence always begins with a capital letter and ends with either a period (.) a question mark (?) or an exclamation point (!).

FUNCTIONS OF SENTENCES

Sentences have three functions:

1. Sentences give information or opinions.

   EXAMPLES

   Dan bought a new record.

   Alexander Graham Bell invented the telephone.

   I believe the Cincinnati Reds are the greatest baseball team of all time.

   Joan is trying to get control of Paul's mind.

2.   Sentences ask questions.

> *EXAMPLES*
> Where are we?
>
> How many moons does the planet Mars have?
>
> Did you find the bottle opener?

3.   Sentences make commands.

> *EXAMPLES*
> Get off my back.
>
> Run to the store and pick up a loaf of bread.
>
> Jump!

● EXERCISE 1

Next to each sentence, put either a *1* if it gives information or opinion, a *2* if it asks a question, or a *3* if it makes a command.

1.   Liz is rotating the tires on her car. 1

2.   Are there any more brownies left? 2

3.   Some people are luckier than others. 1

4.   Come here! 3

5.   Red thinks he knows the best way to fix chicken. 1

6.   Does this college offer a degree in journalism? 2

7.   Go and take a running leap off the nearest bridge. 3

8.   The Panama Canal connects the Caribbean Sea with the Pacific Ocean. 1

9.   Call me sometime. 3

10.   Why is that man laughing? 2

Use the answer key to check your work. Mark the results below. Then discuss any incorrect answers with your instructor. .

No. Correct: . . . .   *No. Incorrect: . . . .*

● EXERCISE 2

Write four sentences of your own that give information or express an opinion.

1. *I really didn't like to* ....

....

2. ....

....

3. ....

....

4. ....

....

Write two sentences of your own that ask questions.

1. ....

....

2. ....

....

Write two sentences of your own that make commands.

1. ....

....

2. ....

Show your work to your instructor. Mark your score below.

No. Correct: ....   *No. Incorrect:* ....

Giving information or opinion is the most common function of sentences. Almost all the sentences in the examples and exercises in this book are the type that give information or opinion. In any exercise asking you to write your own sentences, write the kind that gives information or opinion.

KEY TERMS AND CONCEPTS

The key terms and concepts about sentences are these:

1. Clauses (*main clauses* and *subordinate clauses*) make sentences.

2. Clauses must have both a *subject* and a *verb*.

3. Clauses are different from *phrases*, which do *not* have both a subject and a verb.

4. Conjunctions (*coordinate conjunctions* and *subordinate conjunctions*) join one clause to another clause to make different types of sentences.

5. The three types of sentences (*simple sentences, compound sentences*, and *complex sentences*) are defined by the number and types of clauses they have.

SENTENCES AND CLAUSES

A sentence has one or more *clauses.* There are two types of clauses:
1. Main clauses.
2. Subordinate clauses.

1. A *main clause* can stand alone as a sentence.

   EXAMPLES

   She has red hair.

   The captain ordered the soldiers to start firing.

2. A *subordinate clause* cannot stand alone as a sentence. A subordinate clause is only a fragment of a sentence.

   EXAMPLES

   if the mail carrier delivers the mail before noon

   after the rain stopped

   because I could not wait any longer

   which he always does

● EXERCISE 3

If any of the following clauses can stand alone as a sentence, write *main clause* after it, then capitalize the first word and put a period after the last word. If the clause cannot stand alone as a sentence, write *subordinate clause* after it. (The first two are examples.)

1.   ~~H~~ᴴe opened the door(.)   *main clause*

2.   because a light went on in the house   *subordinate clause*

3.   although some people seem very stupid   ꜱᴜʙᴏʀᴅɪɴᴀᴛᴇ

4.   which was in the closet   Sub

5.   the woman looked carefully at her friend   main

6.   the song rang out clear and hopeful in the night   main

7.   when he wrote his book   sub

8.   the dog bit the mail carrier in the leg   main

9.   My sister came home from the party early last night   main

10. that her old boyfriend started dating her girlfriend Sue   sub

Use the answer key to check your work. Mark the results below. Then discuss any incorrect answers with your instructor.

No. Correct: . . . .   *No. Incorrect:* . . . .

SUBJECTS AND VERBS

Every clause, whether it is a main clause or a subordinate clause, has a *subject* and a *verb* that go together.

EXAMPLES
Main Clauses

        S   V
The customer phoned the store.

        S   V
The manager answered.

s   v
<u>Money</u> is important.

s   v
The <u>game</u> on television <u>ran</u> into overtime.

Subordinate Clauses

s   v
when the <u>sun</u> <u>shines</u>

s v
even though <u>I</u> <u>have</u> no money

s v   v
which <u>she</u> <u>has</u> always <u>wanted</u>

NOTE: The following examples and exercise use only main clauses.

Subjects

The subject of a clause is the person, place, thing, quality, or idea that the clause is about.

EXAMPLES

s
<u>John</u> is laughing. (*John* is the person the clause is about. *John* is the subject of the clause.)

s
The <u>auditorium</u> shook from the vibrations of the electric guitars. (*Auditorium* is the place the clause is about. *Auditorium* is the subject of the clause.)

s
The <u>orange</u> is sweet. (*Orange* is the thing the clause is about. *Orange* is the subject.)

s
<u>Happiness</u> feels good. (*Happiness* is the quality the clause is about. *Happiness* is the subject.)

s
<u>Justice</u> is blind. (*Justice* is the idea the clause is about. *Justice* is the subject.)

s
(<u>You</u>) Jump! (The subject of a command is always *you*. *You* is the person the clause is about.)

Verbs

The verb is the word (or words) that tells the action or condition of its subject. The verb either (1) gives the information or opinion about the subject, (2) asks the question, or (3) makes the command.

> *EXAMPLES*
>
> s   v
> John is laughing. (*Is laughing* tells the action of the subject John. *Is laughing* is the verb of the sentence.)
>
> v   s
> Is the orange sweet? (*Is* asks the question about the condition of the subject. *Is* is the verb.)
>
> s   v
> (You) Jump! (*Jump* commands the action of the sentence.)

● EXERCISE 4

Underline the subject and the verb in each of the following sentences. Mark *s* above the subject and *v* above the verb.

1. The road runs from my house all the way downtown.
2. Are you Millie's sister?
3. The mansion at the top of the hill belongs to the mayor.
4. Open the window.
5. There is a pencil sharpener in the next room.
6. Our team has played winning baseball all year.
7. Love makes everything beautiful.
8. The children love to go swimming.
9. Many famous performers will appear at the coliseum this year.
10. Our neighbors have been planning a trip to California for five years.
11. They have never traveled outside of this city.
12. A good stereo can easily cost six hundred dollars.

13. Does that store carry the best brands?

14. Where did I put the flashlight?

15. To win is everything.

16. The girl standing in the aisle was winking at the drummer.

17. At five o'clock the exhausted workers filed out of the factory.

18. Her friends have exhausted themselves playing tennis.

19. Driven to extreme measures, the crooked politician concealed the evidence of his crimes.

20. If possible, those crazy Calhouns would have driven from Florida to Michigan without stopping.

Show your answers to your instructor. Mark your score below.

No. Correct: . . . .   *No. Incorrect:* . . . .

NOTE: If you had more than three incorrect answers in marking the subjects and the verbs in this exercise, go to page 19 and do all of *Section Two*, Verb Recognition. Then come back here and finish *Section One*.

CLAUSES AND PHRASES

A *clause* is any group of words that has both a subject and a verb. There may be other words in a clause, but it must have at least a subject and a verb.

EXAMPLES
Main Clauses

s   v
Birds fly.

s   v
She has red hair.

s   v
The captain ordered the soldiers to start firing.

Subordinate Clauses

       s   v

after the <u>rain</u> <u>stopped</u>

       s   v

if the <u>mail carrier</u> <u>delivers</u> the mail before noon

       s v   v

because <u>I</u> <u>could</u> not <u>wait</u> any longer

       s   v

which <u>he</u> always <u>does</u>

A *phrase* is any group of words that *does not have* both a subject and a verb. A phrase is only a fragment of a sentence.

EXAMPLES

at the start

the man with the hat

running around the corner

drinking gin and tonic

to tell the truth

on top of her head

struck by a rock

pleased with the gifts

the lady sitting on the bench

might have been planning

These groups of words are phrases because none of them has *both* a subject and a verb.

● EXERCISE 5

If a group of words has a subject and a verb, underline both of them; then capitalize the first word and put a period after the last word. If the group of words does not have both a subject and a verb, write *phrase* after it. (The first two are examples.)

1. T<u>h</u>e <u>paper</u> <u>was</u> on the bed.

2. in the corner behind the table   *phrase*

3. S<u>she</u> <u>answered</u> the telephone.

4. $\overset{P}{}$ $\overset{S}{\underline{dancing}}$ $\overset{\cup}{all}$ night long .

5. $\overset{}{\top}$ the $\overset{S}{announcer}$ read a $\overset{\checkmark}{special}$ news bulletin ·

6.   to be number one   *phrase*

7.   bent out of shape   *phrase*

8. $\overset{}{\top}$ the $\overset{S}{important\ \underline{thing}}$ is to $\overset{\cup}{try}$ your best ,

9. $\overset{}{\text{His}}$ $\overset{S}{\underline{sister}}$ is $\overset{\cup}{playing}$ the trumpet in the parade ,

10. $\overset{}{\top}$ the $\overset{S}{\underline{girl}}$ $\overset{\cup}{standing}$ by the platform ,

Use the answer key to check your work. Mark the results below. Then discuss any incorrect answers with your instructor.

No. Correct: . . . .   *No. Incorrect: . . . .*

CONJUNCTIONS

Conjunctions are joining words.
   One way conjunctions function is to join one clause to another clause to make different types of sentences.
   There are two types of conjunctions:

>   1.   Coordinate conjunctions.
>
>   *EXAMPLES*
>   and   but   so
>
>   2.   Subordinate conjunctions.
>
>   *EXAMPLES*
>   when   even though   which

1.   Coordinate conjunctions join one main clause to another main clause.

.   *EXAMPLES*
(The coordinate conjunctions have boxes around them.)

The customer phoned the store $\boxed{\text{and}}$ the manager answered.
              main clause   main clause

. Money is important $\boxed{\text{but}}$ it is not everything.
        main clause   main clause

> The game on television ran into overtime [so] the next program
>   main clause   main clause
> started late.

2. Subordinate conjunctions join a subordinate clause to a main clause. The subordinate conjunction comes at the *beginning* of the subordinate clause.

   EXAMPLES
   (The subordinate conjunctions have boxes around them.)

   [When] the sun shines, people are happy.
   subordinate clause   main clause

   I feel like a king [even though] I have no money.
      main clause   subordinate clause

   Darlessa bought a red sportscar, [which] she has always wanted.
          main clause   subordinate clause

● EXERCISE 6

In the following sentences, put a box around each coordinate conjunction and each subordinate conjunction. Underline each clause and write either *main clause* or *subordinate clause* under it.

1. The chairs look comfortable [but] they feel hard.
2. Peggy dived into the pool [while] Rose watched her.
3. Mrs. Smith loaned me five dollars [and] I will repay her next Friday.
4. [When] Leon tries his hardest, he is always successful.
5. Diane did a lot of work [which] no one else could have done.
6. John talked too quickly [so] Mary asked him to slow down.

Use the answer key to check your work. Mark the results below. Then discuss any incorrect answers with your instructor.

No. Correct: . . . .   *No. Incorrect:* . . . .

TYPES OF SENTENCES

According to grammatical construction, there are three types of sentences. These three types of sentences are defined according to the number and types of clauses they have.

1. Simple sentences.
   A simple sentence has *one main clause.*

2. Compound sentences.
   A compound sentence has *two or more main clauses.*

3. Complex sentences.
   A complex sentence has at least *one main clause* and at least *one subordinate clause.*

If a group of words does not fit one of these three categories, it is not a grammatically correct sentence.

Simple Sentences

A main clause by itself is the same thing as a simple sentence.

> *EXAMPLES*
>
> s   v
> She has red hair.
>
>   s   v
> The captain ordered the soldiers to start firing.

A main clause may have other words or phrases in it, but it *must* have a subject and a verb.

● EXERCISE 7

Underline the subjects and verbs in the following *simple sentences.* Mark s above the subject and *v* above the verb. (The first one is an example.)

   s   v
1. Jane walked quietly through the front door.

     s   o
2. The boy rode his motorcycle into the curb.

    s   v
3. Dr. Peer charged four hundred dollars for the plastic surgery.

     s   v
4. The airplane waiting to land cruised at nine thousand feet above the city.

     s   v
5. Elaine's husband gave her a diamond watch for her birthday.

Use the answer key to check your work. Mark the results below. Then discuss any incorrect answers with your instructor.

No. Correct: . . . .   *No. Incorrect:* . . . .

● EXERCISE 8

Write three simple sentences of your own.

1. *Doc scored 27 point last game*

2. *John ran a 4 minute mile early this morning*

3. *The race will begin in a few minutes*

Show your work to your instructor. Mark your score below.

No. Correct: . . . .   *No. Incorrect:* . . . .

Compound Sentences

A compound sentence has *two or more main clauses.* Therefore it is like two simple sentences joined together. The most common way to join two simple sentences to make a compound sentence is to use a *coordinate conjunction.*

> *EXAMPLES*
>
> S   V   S   V
> She has red hair but her sister has brown hair.
>
> S   V   S   V
> The children went to the ice cream shop and they bought double-decker cones.

A semicolon (;) can also be used to join two simple sentences into a compound sentence.

> *EXAMPLES*
>
> S   V   S   V
> The airplanes made a terrible racket; they disturbed my concentration.
>
> S   V   S
> The captain ordered the soldiers to start firing; however, they
> V
> refused to obey the order.

● EXERCISE 9

Put a box around the coordinating conjunction (or semicolon) in the following *compound sentences.* Underline the subjects and verbs and mark *s* above the subject and *v* above the verb. (Remember to look for two subjects and verbs in each sentence.) The first one is an example.

1. They won the battle but they lost the war.

2. Richard ate too much so his stomach felt bloated.

3. She called him once more and he told her not to call again.

4. They sold the store but they hung on to the house.

5. The mail carrier is coming; you should bring the dog in.

Use the answer key to check your work. Mark the results below. Then discuss any incorrect answers with your instructor.

No. Correct: . . . .   *No. Incorrect:* . . . .

● EXERCISE 10

Write three compound sentences of your own.

1. *Joe will be hear at 8:00 and Jill will be along later*

2. *The ...*

3.

Show your work to your instructor. Mark your score below.

No. Correct: . . . .   *No. Incorrect:* . . . .

Complex Sentences

A complex sentence has at least *one main clause* and at least *one subordinate clause*. Each subordinate clause begins with a *subordinate conjunction*.

EXAMPLES
(Each subordinate clause is underlined. Each subordinate conjunction has a box around it.)

| After | the rain stopped, we went on a picnic.

I gave up on Larry | because | I could not wait any longer.

She wore the necklace | that | she inherited from her grandmother.

The horse was a champion; but | because | it broke its leg, the owner put it to sleep.

| Although | the whole family was eating dinner, nobody saw the fly | that | landed in the dish of butter.

A complex sentence is the *only* type of sentence that has a *subordinate clause* in it.

● EXERCISE 11

Put a box around the subordinate conjunction at the beginning of each subordinate clause in the following *complex sentences*. Underline the subjects and verbs in both the main clauses and the subordinate clauses. Mark *s* above the subject and *v* above the verb. (Remember to look for two subjects and verbs in each sentence.) The first one is an example.

1. He stared at me | as if | I were a convicted murderer.

2. | Until | you get him angry, Larry is a lot of fun.

3. He spoke in silver tones to the woman | who | was smiling at him.

4. The lonely man drove to the beach | where | he walked for hours along the water's edge.

5. When Sharon heard about the accident, she broke into tears that flowed for hours.

Use the answer key to check your work. Mark the results below. Then discuss any incorrect answers with your instructor.

No. Correct: . . . .   *No. Incorrect:* . . . .

● EXERCISE 12

Write three complex sentences of your own.

1. . . . .

. . . .

. . . .

2. . . . .

. . . .

. . . .

3. . . . .

. . . .

. . . .

Show your work to your instructor. Mark your score below.

No. Correct: . . . .   *No. Incorrect:* . . . .

Review: Sentence Fundamentals

This section introduces all the key terms and concepts you need to know in order to understand and write grammatically correct sentences. The key terms are:

Subject
Verb
Phrase
Clause
    Main Clause
    Subordinate Clause

Conjunction
    Coordinate Conjunction
    Subordinate Conjunction
Sentence
    Simple Sentence
    Compound Sentence
    Complex Sentence

The following key concepts about sentences explain the relationships of the key terms:

Every *clause* has a *subject* and a *verb.*

A *main clause* can stand alone as a *sentence.*

A *subordinate clause* cannot stand alone as a sentence.

A *phrase* does not have a subject and a verb and therefore a phrase cannot stand alone as a sentence.

A *simple sentence* has *one main clause.*

EXAMPLE

  s   v
She has red hair.
   main clause

A *compound sentence* has *two or more main clauses,* which are most commonly joined by a *coordinate conjunction.*

EXAMPLE

  s   v   s   v
She has red hair [but] her sister has brown hair.
   main clause   main clause

A *complex sentence* has at least *one main clause* and at least *one subordinate clause.* Each subordinate clause begins with a *subordinate conjunction.*

EXAMPLE

           s   v   s   v
[After] the rain stopped, we went on a picnic.
  subordinate clause   main clause

The remaining sections of this book explain the key terms and related matters in detail and give you the opportunity to work with them until you master them. Then you will be able to write grammatically correct sentences whenever you want to.

● EXERCISE 13: REVIEW

In the following sentences, mark *s* above each subject and *v* above each verb.
If the sentence has only one main clause, write *simple sentence* after it. Put a
box around the *coordinate conjunction* in the compound sentences and
around the *subordinate conjunction* in the complex sentences. If the sentence
has two or more main clauses, write *compound sentence* after it. If the sentence has one main clause and at least one subordinate clause, write *complex
sentence* after it. (The first three items are examples.)

1. ⌷Because⌷ the house caught fire, somebody called for help.
   complex sentence

2. In spite of the help of the firemen, the house burned down.
   simple sentence

3. The house has burned down ⌷and⌷ the family must move in with relatives.
   compound sentence

4. The falling leaves have many colors, ⌷but⌷ the most common color is gold.

5. Robert is licking the tips of the rose with his tongue.

6. ⌷When⌷ their favorite driver won the race, the crowd cheered.

7. On Tuesday the plumber finally responded to the call which we made
   early last week.

8. He will unclog the stopped-up drain.

9. The clock on the wall says twelve, but my watch says five after twelve.

10. Although the odds are against us, we can succeed.

Use the answer key to check your work. Mark the results below. Then discuss
any incorrect answers with your instructor.

No. Correct: . . . .   *No. Incorrect:* . . . .

You have completed *Section One.* Now go on to *Section Three*,
Sentence Elements, p. 57.

SECTION TWO

Verb Recognition

FINDING THE SUBJECT AND VERB

Subject and verb always go together in a sentence. You can't have one without the other.

Although the subject usually comes first, it is best to try to find the verb first. The verb is the most important part of the sentence. All the other words in the sentence are built around the verb.

Step One: Find the Verb

Look for the word (or words) that tells an action or condition.

EXAMPLES

Betty smiles often. (*Smiles* is the verb. It tells an action.)

The canary was singing all day. (*Was singing* is the verb. It tells an action.)

The shoes feel comfortable. (*Feel* is the verb. It tells a condition.)

The green hat is on the shelf. (*Is* is the verb. It tells a condition.)

Step Two: Find the Subject

Ask *who?* or *what?* and repeat the verb. The answer to this question is the subject.

> *EXAMPLES*
>
> v
> Betty smiles often. (*Who or what smiles? The answer is Betty. Betty is the subject.*)
>
> v
> The canary was singing all day. (*Who or what was singing? The answer is canary. Canary is the subject.*)
>
> v
> The shoes feel comfortable. (*Who or what feels? The answer is shoes. Shoes is the subject.*)
>
> v
> The green hat is on the shelf. (*Who or what is? The answer is hat. Hat is the subject.*)

Use this method to find the subject and the verb in the following exercises.

● EXERCISE 14

Underline the subject and the verb in each of the following sentences. Mark *s* above the subject and *v* above the verb. Look for the verb first.

       s   v
1. The student did his assignment.

     s   v
2. John was studying French.

      s   v
3. The house stands on a corner lot.

     s   v
4. The water feels warm.

    s   v
5. Mother is sewing the skirt for Barbara.

     s   v
6. The apples on the table look rotten.

Use the answer key to check your work. Mark the results below. Then discuss any incorrect answers with your instructor.

No. Correct: . . . .   No. Incorrect: . . . .

VERB RECOGNITION: EIGHT WAYS TO RECOGNIZE A VERB

Verbs are complicated and they are not always easy to recognize.
But it is very important to be able to find the verb, because the rest of
the sentence is built around the verb. This section will show you eight
ways to recognize verbs.

1. Recognize a verb by its meaning.

2. Recognize a verb by the fact that it goes with a subject.

3. Recognize a verb by its position after its subject.

4. Recognize a verb by its many changes of form.

5. Recognize a verb by its time function.

6. Recognize verb phrases.

7. Recognize words that are always verbs.

8. Recognize a verb by telling it apart from a verbal.

Recognize a Verb by Its Meaning

Verbs are words that:
1. mean an action, or
2. mean a condition or state of being.

EXAMPLES

Action Verbs

sing	think	accept
run	write	imagine

Condition (State of Being) Verbs

am	seem
is	become
are	
was	
were	

● EXERCISE 15

Next to each of the following words write *v* if it can be used as a verb or *nv* if it is not a verb.

1. buy

2. heart

3. embarrass

4. was

5. food

6. see

7. cigarette

8. feel

9. eat

10. quickly

Use the answer key to check your work. Mark the results below. Then discuss any incorrect answers with your instructor.

No. Correct: . . . .   *No. Incorrect:* . . . .

You cannot always tell just by looking at a word by itself whether or not it is a verb. Many words function in different ways in different sentences. For example, a word can be the verb in one sentence and the subject in another sentence.

EXAMPLES

s   v
I love you. (Here *love* is the verb.)

    s   v
Our love is beautiful. (Here *love* is the subject of the verb *is.*)

   s   v
You smoke too much. (Here *smoke* is the verb.)

   s   v
Smoke filled the room (Here *smoke* is the subject of the verb *filled.*)

With a word that can function either as a subject or a verb, you have to see how it is used in the particular sentence to tell for sure what it is.

● EXERCISE 16

In the following pairs of sentences, the same word is used once as a subject and once as a verb. Mark *s* above the subject and *v* above the verb in each sentence.

1. Tina's laugh makes everybody happy.

   Some people always laugh at the wrong time.

2. Those sisters talk on the phone every night.

   The mayor's talk on police brutality was controversial.

3. The cause of the flooding was a sudden thunderstorm.

   Sudden thunderstorms cause flooding.

4. Your first thought is often your best.

   The president thought like a criminal.

5. The problems of inflation and recession concern everyone.

   Bob's main concern is unemployment.

Use the answer key to check your work. Mark the results below. Then discuss any incorrect answers with your instructor.

No. Correct: . . . .   *No. Incorrect:* . . . .

● EXERCISE 17

For each of the following words, write two sentences. In the first sentence use the word as the *subject*; in the second sentence use the same word as a *verb*.

1. dream   (a) . . . .

   . . . .

   (b) . . . .

   . . . .

2. work   (a) ....

                         ....

                         (b) ....

                         ....

3. hate   (a) ....

                         ....

                         (b) ....

                         ....

4. drink   (a) ....

                         ....

                         (b) ....

                         ....

5. pitch   (a) ....

                         ....

                         (b) ....

                         ....

Show your work to your instructor. Mark your score below.

No. Correct: ....   *No. Incorrect:* ....

Recognize a Verb by the Fact That It Goes with a Subject

A subject and a verb always go together in a sentence. You cannot have one without the other. A subject always has a verb; and, vice versa, a verb always has a subject.

EXAMPLES

        s   v
The clock ticks constantly.

    s   v
She is here.

s   v
The bartender smiled at Lili.

In a sentence the subject and the verb relate to each other *in meaning,* even though other words may come in between.

EXAMPLES

s   v
The <u>clock</u> on the wall <u>ticks</u> constantly.

s   v
The <u>bartender</u> at the discotheque <u>smiled</u> at Lili.

s   v
The <u>color</u> of the rose <u>was</u> red.

NOTE: Although it is true that roses are red, the subject of this last sentence is *color* not *rose.*

● EXERCISE 18

Underline the subject and the verb in each of the following sentences. Mark *s* above the subject and *v* above the verb.

1. We caught the last bus home.

2. I buy food at the local supermarket.

3. The texture of the cloth is smooth.

4. The book on sex techniques looks interesting.

5. Her dinners taste delicious.

6. The girls in the dorm expected a party tonight.

7. He worries about everything.

8. The sound of the trumpets hurt my ears.

Use the answer key to check your work. Mark the results below. Then discuss any incorrect answers with your instructor.

No. Correct: . . . .   *No. Incorrect:* . . . .

Recognize a Verb by Its Position after Its Subject

In sentences that give information or opinions, the verb comes *after* its subject. But this does not mean that the verb always comes immediately after the subject; any number of other words may come between them.

EXAMPLES

s   v
The sun shines brightly.

s   v
The sun always shines brightly.

s v
The old tree fell down.

s   v
The old tree in my front yard fell down.

s v
Hattie loves Pete.

s   v
Hattie, a warm and passionate girl, loves Pete.

s v
The boy tripped on a rock

s   v
The boy, running across the parking lot, tripped on a rock.

NOTE: In each pair of examples, the subject and verb remain the same, even though in the second sentence a number of other words come in between the subject and the verb.

● EXERCISE 19

Underline the subject and the verb in each of the following sentences. Mark *s* above the subject and *v* above the verb.

1. Betty met Bob.

2. Betty, a bright and charming person, liked Bob, an equally bright and charming person, immediately.

3. Betty had three children from a previous marriage.

4. She proudly told Bob about her children.

5. Bob, like Betty, also had children from a previous marriage.

6. The children at first hated each other.

7. Bob, losing his temper, punished them.

8. Betty, being more understanding, taught them games to play.

9. The children finally learned how to get along with each other.

10. Now everyone is happy.

Use the answer key to check your work. Mark the results below. Then discuss any incorrect anwswer with your instructor.

No. Correct: . . . .   *No. Incorrect:* . . . .

Exceptions to the Rule of Position

In sentences that begin with *there is, there are,* or *here is, here are,* the verb comes *before* its subject.

> *EXAMPLES*
>
>   v   s
> There are three children in the yard.
>
>   v   s
> Here is the record.

Also in sentences that ask a question the verb comes *before* its subject.

> *EXAMPLES*
>
>   v   s
> Are you sad?
>
>   v   s
> Is Calvin your brother?

● EXERCISE 20

Underline the subject and the verb in each of the following sentences. Mark *s* above the subject and *v* above the verb.

1. People are in that room.

2. There are people in that room.

3. Here is the book.

4. The book is here on the table.

5. This rule has an exception.

6. There is an exception to this rule.

7. Are you angry?

8. Is everyone ready?

Use the answer key to check your work. Mark the results below. Then discuss any incorrect answers with your instructor.

No. Correct: . . . .   *No. Incorrect: . . . .*

_____

Recognize a Verb by Its Many Changes of Form

Verbs change their form more than any other words in the English language.

EXAMPLE

verb: <u>jump</u>

jumps	am jumping	jumped
will jump	is jumping	has jumped
did jump	was jumping	have jumped
can jump	could be jumping	would have jumped

Those are only some forms of the verb *jump.*

If you can change any word in the ways *jump* was changed, then that word can function as a verb in a sentence.

EXAMPLES

kiss: Can the word *kiss* be a verb?

kisses	am kissing	kissed
will kiss	is kissing	has kissed

Yes, *kiss* can be a verb, because it can change form in those ways.

see: Can the word *see* be a verb?

sees	am seeing	saw
will see	is seeing	has seen

Yes, *see* can be a verb, because it can change form in those ways.

door: Can the word *door* be a verb?

doors	am dooring	doored
will door	is dooring	has doored

No, *door* cannot be a verb, because changing *door* in those ways does not make sense.

● EXERCISE 21

See if the following words can be verbs by making the changes in form as shown in the examples above. Put *v* next to the word if it can be a verb. Put *nv* next to it if it is not a verb. (The first item is an example.)

1. taste **V**   tastes   am tasting   tasted
    will taste   is tasting   has tasted

2. help   . . . .
             . . . .

3. desk   . . . .
             . . . .

4. accept   . . . .
             . . . .

5. feel   . . . .
             . . . .

6. rapidly . . . .
             . . . .

7. think   . . . .
             . . . .

8. about   . . . .
             . . . .

9. beautiful   . . . .
   . . . .

10. believe   . . . .
    . . . .

11. his   . . . .
    . . . .

12. sit   . . . .
    . . . .

13. into   . . . .
    . . . .

14. trip   . . . .
    . . . .

15. happy   . . . .
    . . . .

Use the answer key to check your work. Mark the results below. Then discuss any incorrect answers with your instructor.

No. Correct: . . . .   *No. Incorrect:* . . . .

● EXERCISE 22: REVIEW

Underline the subject and the verb in each of the following sentences. Mark *s* above the subject and *v* above the verb.

1. The girl in the blue-and-white jersey ran the winning race.

2. They run twenty miles a week for practice.

3. A run in her pantyhose embarrassed her.

4. Jim's new job excites him.

5. There is a stray dog in the yard.

6. Is your brother in the army?

7. The vegetables from our garden taste delicious.

Use the answer key to check your work. Mark the results below. Then discuss any incorrect answers with your instructor.

No. Correct: . . . .   *No. Incorrect:* . . . .

Recognize a Verb by Its Time Function

A verb tells the time of the action or condition of its subject.

The three basic times of verbs are the *present*, the *past*, and the *future*. Verbs change form to show the different times.

EXAMPLES

Present Tense	Past Tense	Future Tense
I dance.	I danced.	I will dance.
She is sorry.	She was sorry.	She will be sorry.

Tense refers to the time function of verbs. There are twelve tenses (times) for each verb in English. There are four different tenses for each of the basic times, *present*, *past*, and *future*.

EXAMPLES
The twelve tenses of the verbs *vote* and *take*:

I. SIMPLE TENSES

1. *Present*
   We vote in November
   Sarah takes a taxi.

2. *Past*
   We voted in November.
   Sarah took a taxi.

3. *Future*
   We will vote in November.
   Sarah will take a taxi.

II. PROGRESSIVE TENSES

4. *Present Progressive*
   We are voting in November.
   Sarah is taking a taxi.

5. *Past Progressive*
   We were voting in November.
   Sarah was taking a taxi.

6. *Future Progressive*
   We will be voting in November.
   Sarah will be taking a taxi.

III. PERFECT TENSES	*IV. PERFECT PROGRESSIVE TENSES*
7. Present Perfect We <u>have voted</u> in November. Sarah <u>has taken</u> a taxi.	*10. Present Perfect Progressive* We <u>have been voting</u> in November. Sarah <u>has been taking</u> a taxi.
8. Past Perfect We <u>had voted</u> in November. Sarah <u>had taken</u> a taxi.	*11. Past Perfect Progressive* We <u>had been voting</u> in November. Sarah <u>had been taking</u> a taxi.
9. Future Perfect We <u>will have voted</u> in November. Sarah <u>will have taken</u> a taxi.	*12. Future Perfect Progressive* (This form is not often used.) We <u>will have been voting</u> in November. Sarah <u>will have been taking</u> a taxi.

Note that the four categories of tenses come in *present*, *past*, and *future*.

● EXERCISE 23

Underline the subject and the verb in each of the following sentences. Change the form of each verb to a different tense, either *present*, *past*, or *future*.

1. We talk about movies on Friday night.

2. Mr. Taylor worked as an orderly in a hospital.

3. The twins splashed water all over the bathroom floor.

4. The dogs in the alley bark at cats all night long.

5. My sister bought a silver tray for our parents' anniversary.

6. Her experiences as a child influenced her adult behavior.

7. The spaceship will leave the earth's atmosphere.

Show your work to your instructor. Mark your score below.

No. Correct: . . . .   *No. Incorrect:* . . . .

Recognize Verb Phrases

By now you will have noticed that some verb forms have only one word, while others have two, three, or more words. If you look at the list of twelve tenses for the verbs *vote* and *take* (starting on p. 31), you will see that only the *simple present tense* and the *simple past tense* have one word. All the other forms have two or more words. Verb forms with more than one word are called *verb phrases.*

> *EXAMPLES*
>
> are doing　　　　have voted　　　　will have broken
>
> will go　　　　　has been talking　　would have been chosen

Definition: **Verb Phrase**

A verb phrase is two or more words that together are the verb. Every verb phrase consists of the *main verb* and one or more *helping verbs* in front of the main verb.

> *EXAMPLES*
>
> will come (*come* is the main verb; *will* is the helping verb)
>
> have been climbing (*climbing* is the main verb; *have* and *been* are helping verbs)
>
> may have talked (*talked* is the main verb; *may* and *have* are helping verbs)

NOTE: The *main verb* is always the *last* word in a verb phrase. When you are asked to find the verb, be sure to find *the whole verb phrase.*

● EXERCISE 24

Underline the subject and the verb in each of the following sentences. If the verb has more than one word, put two lines under the main verb.

1. We talked last night.

2. We will be there on time.

3. John has gone to school for twelve years.

4. They have been dancing for five hours.

5. The man in the sweater is looking for you.

6. Those girls were in our class last year.

7. By spring, I will have been living here for ten years.

8. The Simpsons have gone to California for the holidays.

Use the answer key to check your work. Mark the results below. Then discuss
any incorrect answers with your instructor.

No. Correct: . . . .   *No. Incorrect:* . . . .

Interrupted Verb Phrases

Verb phrases may be interrupted by other words. These other words
separate a helping verb from the rest of the verb phrase.

> *EXAMPLES*
>
> The sun is not shining today. (*Not* separates the helping verb
>   *is* from the main verb *shining*; *is shining* is the whole verb
>   phrase.)
>
> We don't have any gas. (*N't* separates the helping verb *do* from
>   the main verb *have*; *do have* is the whole verb phrase.)
>
> We will easily catch that bus. (*Will catch* is the whole verb
>   phrase.)
>
> Louise and Ron were, on at least two different Saturday nights,
>   skating on the lake. (*Were skating* is the whole verb phrase.)

In questions, too, the main verb is separated from the helping verb. In
these cases it usually is the subject that separates the two parts of the
helping verb.

> *EXAMPLES*
>
>   s
> Are you going to church?
>
>   s
> Did Bob find his watch?
>
>   s
> Have the neighbors in the next apartment stopped their noise?

When you are asked to find the verb in a sentence, be sure to find the
whole verb phrase.

● EXERCISE 25

Mark *s* above the subject in each of the following sentences. Put one line under the helping verb and two lines under the main verb.

1. Kennedy is not running for president.

2. Mary is definitely going to New York soon.

3. The children didn't have any candy.

4. The policemen were relentlessly interrogating my friend.

5. Steve would, on almost every weekend, drink way too much wine.

6. Have they lost their way?

7. Is Toby running in the race Saturday?

8. Does your friend from California know any famous celebrities?

9. Last winter, did you have the flu?

10. Has the repairman called yet?

Use the answer key to check your work. Mark the results below. Then discuss any incorrect answers with your instructor.

No. Correct: . . . .   *No. Incorrect:* . . . .

Recognize Words That Are Always Verbs

Some words are *always* verbs. Memorize them.

WORDS THAT ARE ALWAYS VERBS

am	do	have
is	does	has
are	did	had
was		
were		

The words in this list can be verbs by themselves in sentences or they can be helping verbs.

> *EXAMPLE*
>
> I am ready.
>
> I am leaving now.
>
> She does her best.
>
> She does love you.
>
> They had fish for dinner.
>
> They had tried everything.

NOTE: In each pair of examples, the same word is first a verb by itself and then a helping verb.

● EXERCISE 26

Mark *s* above the subject in each of the following sentences. Underline the verb. If there is more than one word to the verb, put two lines under the main verb.

1. I am glad for you.

2. I am borrowing your chairs for the party.

3. Mary did the assignment correctly.

4. John did not do the assignment at all.

5. They have worked hard for their living.

6. His sister's family has a new home.

7. There was a book on the table by the bed.

8. The members of the union were voting on the contract.

Use the answer key to check your work. Mark the results below. Then discuss any incorrect answers with your instructor.

No. Correct: . . . .   *No. Incorrect:* . . . .

● EXERCISE 27

For each of the following words write two sentences of your own. In the first sentence, use the word as a verb by itself. In the second sentence, use the word as a helping verb. (The first item is an example.)

1. is   (a)   That man <u>is</u> the owner of the restaurant.

         (b)   Sharon <u>is planning</u> a new career.

2. are   (a) . . . .

         (b) . . . .

3. does (a) . . . .

         (b) . . . .

4. was (a) . . . .

         (b) . . . .

5. has (a) . . . .

         (b) . . . .

Show your work to your instructor. Mark your score below.

No. Correct: . . . .   *No. Incorrect:* . . . .

WORDS THAT ARE ALWAYS
HELPING VERBS

shall	would	may
must	should	
	could	

EXAMPLES

John <u>must behave</u> himself.

Mary <u>could win</u> the championship.

WORDS THAT ARE ALMOST ALWAYS
HELPING VERBS

will	can	might

EXAMPLES

I will go first.

You can follow me.

We might make it.

(Here are some examples where these words *are not* verbs:
free *will;* tin *can;* the *might* of God.)

● EXERCISE 28

Mark *s* above the subject in each of the following sentences. Underline the verb. If there is more than one word to the verb, put two lines under the main verb.

1. I might come to your house later.

2. You must answer all the questions on the exam.

3. They could have found the answer by themselves.

4. Your goal is reasonable.

5. We can surely find a substitute.

6. Does Maisie have my keys in her purse?

7. The flowers in the garden will bloom again next year.

8. The children have been playing in the water all day.

Use the answer key to check your work. Mark the results below. Then discuss any incorrect answers with your instructor.

No. Correct: . . . .   *No. Incorrect:* . . . .

● EXERCISE 29

Write a sentence of your own for each of the following words. Underline the whole verb phrase.

1. should   ....

   ....

2. may   ....

   ....

3. will   ....

   ....

4. could   ....

   ....

5. might   ....

   ....

Show your work to your instructor. Mark your score below.

No. Correct: ....   *No. Incorrect:* ....

Recognize a Verb by Telling It apart from Verbals

Some words look like verbs but they do not function as verbs in sentences. These words are made from verbs and they are easy to confuse with verbs. These words are called *verbals*.

There are three kinds of verbals:
1. Infinitives.
2. Gerunds.
3. Participles.

Infinitives

Infinitives are made up of the word *to* and the root form of a verb.

EXAMPLES

to dance	to think	to be
to speak	to try	to act

NOTE: An infinitive *never* functions as a verb in a sentence.

● EXERCISE 30

Underline the subject and verb in each of the following sentences. Put parentheses around each infinitive. (The first item is an example.)

1. <u>Children</u> <u>like</u> (to laugh) a lot.

2. The girl in the pink dress promised to try harder.

3. You have to work hard for a good salary.

4. The workers are trying to do a good job.

5. Mike wants to kiss Cathy.

6. To win is not the only thing worthwhile.

7. Well-prepared people find jobs easy to get.

Use the answer key to check your work. Mark the results below. Then discuss any incorrect answers with your instructor.

No. Correct: . . . .   *No. Incorrect:* . . . .

● EXERCISE 31

Write a sentence cf your own using each of the following infinitives.

1. to taste   . . . .

  . . . .

2. to do   . . . .

  . . . .

3. to be ....

....

4. to cry ....

....

Show your work to your instructor. Mark your score below.

No. Correct: ....   *No. Incorrect:* ....

Gerunds

A gerund is made by adding *ing* to the root form of a verb.

EXAMPLES

Root	*Gerund*
talk	talk*ing*
want	want*ing*
be	be*ing*
ring	ring*ing*

If the root form ends in a silent *e*, drop the *e* and add *ing*.

EXAMPLES

Root	*Gerund*
rid*e*	rid*ing*
tast*e*	tast*ing*

If the root form ends in a single consonant preceded by a single vowel, double the consonant and add *ing*.

EXAMPLES

Root	*Gerund*
grab	gra*bb*ing
beg	be*gg*ing
hit	hi*tt*ing
swim	swi*mm*ing

● EXERCISE 32

Make a gerund out of each of the following verbs by adding *ing*. (Drop a silent *e* or double a consonant, if necessary.)

1. sing . . . .   6. run   . . . .

2. drive . . . .   7. bite   . . . .

3. sit   . . . .   8. trip   . . . .

4. stab . . . .   9. hide   . . . .

5. think . . . .   10. see   . . . .

Use the answer key to check your work. Mark the results below. Then discuss any incorrect answers with your instructor.

No. Correct: . . . .   *No. Incorrect:* . . . .

A gerund is used as a subject in a sentence.

> **EXAMPLES**
>
> s   v
> Swimming is good exercise.
>
> s   v
> Learning grammar is difficult.
>
> s   v
> Trying hard brings success.

NOTE: Gerunds are *never* used as verbs.

● EXERCISE 33

Underline the subject and the verb in each of the following sentences. Mark *s* above the subject and *v* above the verb.

1. Smoking does terrible things to your lungs.

2. Running is the best exercise.

3. Seeing you again is making me happy.

4.   Smiling encourages friendliness.

Use the answer key to check your work. Mark the results below. Then discuss any incorrect answers with your instructor.

No. Correct: . . . .   *No. Incorrect:* . . . .

● EXERCISE 34

Write a sentence of your own using each of the following gerunds as the subject.

1.   dancing   . . . .

. . . .

2.   thinking   . . . .

. . . .

3.   beginning   . . . .

. . . .

4.   driving   . . . .

. . . .

Show your work to your instructor. Mark your score below.

No. Correct: . . . .   *No. Incorrect:* . . . .

Participles

Participles are the most complicated kind of verbal. This section will explain how to make participles and how to use participles in their different complicated ways.

There are two kinds of participles:

1.   The present participle.
2.   The past participle.

Present Participle

The present participle is made the same way that a gerund is made. Add *ing* to the root form of the verb.

EXAMPLES

Root	*Present Participle*
bring	bring*ing*
eat	eat*ing*

(drop silent *e*)

slid*e*	slid*ing*
dar*e*	dar*ing*

(double consonant)

dri*p*	dri*pp*ing
hu*m*	hu*mm*ing

● EXERCISE 35

Make a present participle out of each of the following verbs by adding *ing*. (Drop a silent *e* or double a consonant, if necessary.)

1. speak	. . . .	6. hope	. . . .
2. hire	. . . .	7. drop	. . . .
3. shut	. . . .	8. do	. . . .
4. shout	. . . .	9. try	. . . .
5. cling	. . . .	10. have	. . . .

Use the answer key to check your work. Mark the results below. Then discuss any incorrect answers with your instructor.

No. Correct: . . . .   *No. Incorrect:* . . . .

The present participle by itself never functions as a verb in a sentence. Here are some examples of ways present participles do function.

EXAMPLES

                      S   V

The <u>shouting</u> children suddenly became quiet.

      s   v

The woman <u>speaking</u> to her husband lost her temper.

       s   v

<u>Walking</u> slowly, Connie was deep in thought.

● EXERCISE 36

Underline the present participles in the following sentences. Mark *s* above the subject and *v* above the verb. (The first three items are examples.)

          s   v

1. The <u>burning</u> skyscraper became a <u>towering</u> inferno.

     s   v

2. The man <u>eating</u> the enormous ice cream sundae was extremely fat.

          s v

3. <u>Having</u> nothing to do, Betty went to a movie.

4. Gregory, being a hard worker, always succeeds in his work.

5. The barking dogs kept my friend awake all night.

6. Linda, shutting the door behind her, walked towards the bed.

7. Going slowly down the street, Anna noticed every sign of life.

8. Running barefoot through the park, Jerome cut himself on some broken glass.

9. The speeding car turned the corner sharply.

10. The nervous man sat smoking one cigarette after another.

Use the answer key to check your work. Mark the results below. Then discuss any incorrect answers with your instructor.

No. Correct: . . . .   *No. Incorrect:* . . . .

A present participle can be a verb if it has a helping verb in front of it.

EXAMPLES

The swaying branches are graceful. (*Swaying* is not a verb
because it does not have a helping verb in front of it.)

The branches are swaying in the wind. (*Are swaying* is a verb.
Are is the helping verb and *swaying* is the main verb.)

● EXERCISE 37

If a word or group of words can be a verb, write *v* next to it. If it cannot be a
verb, write *nv* next to it.

1. having

2. will be having

3. being

4. was going

5. coming

6. was having

7. were being

8. going

9. is

10. have been coming

Use the answer key to check your work. Mark the results below. Then discuss
any incorrect answers with your instructor.

No. Correct: . . . .   *No. Incorrect:* . . . .

● EXERCISE 38

Underline the subject and the verb in each of the following sentences. Put
parentheses around any present participle that is not part of a verb phrase.
(The first two items are examples.)

1. (Being) full of energy, the children played games all afternoon.

2. They are being a nuisance on purpose.

3. At dawn the birds were chirping in the trees.

4. The birds chirping outside my window woke me pleasantly.

5. Her sparkling eyes attracted attention.

6. They were having a wonderful time at the party.

7. He has been coming to dinner at my house for years.

8. Turning the corner, Lili saw Charles waiting for her.

9. The dancer was spinning on her toes.

10. He was being stubborn out of pride.

Use the answer key to check your work. Mark the results below. Then discuss any incorrect answers with your instructor.

No. Correct: . . . .   *No. Incorrect:* . . . .

● EXERCISE 39

Write a sentence of your own for each of the following words. Underline the subject and the verb in your sentence.

1. going   . . . .

     . . . .

2. opening   . . . .

     . . . .

3. closing   . . . .

     . . . .

4. hitting   . . . .

     . . . .

5. trying   . . . .

     . . . .

Show your work to your instructor. Mark your score below.

No. Correct: . . . .   *No. Incorrect:* . . . .

Past Participle

Regular Verbs

The past participle of *regular verbs* is made the same way as the past tense is made, by adding *d* or *ed* to the root form of the verb.

> *EXAMPLES*
>
> | *Root* | *Past Participle* |
> |--------|-------------------|
> | smoke | smoke*d* |
> | create | create*d* |
> | return | return*ed* |
> | destroy| destroy*ed* |

By itself the past participle never functions as a verb in a sentence. Here are some examples of ways past participles do function.

> *EXAMPLES*
>
>   s   v
> Smoked salmon is expensive.
>
>   s   v
> That city, destroyed by an earthquake in 1973, is now pros-
>   perous again.

But the past participle can be a verb if it has a helping verb in front of it.

> *EXAMPLES*
>
>   s   v
> Robert has smoked since the fourth grade.
>
>   s   v
> The city was destroyed by an earthquake.

Since both the past tense and the past participle of regular verbs end in *d* or *ed*, the past participle is easily confused with the past tense. They look exactly the same. But the past tense is a verb by itself.

> *EXAMPLES*
>
>   s   v
> She smoked her last cigarette.
>
>   s   v
> A fire destroyed the factory.

● EXERCISE 40

Underline the subject and the verb in each of the following sentences. Put parentheses around any past participle that is not part of a verb phrase. (The first two items are examples.)

1. Mary is my (trusted) friend.

2. Unfortunately the president has trusted the wrong man.

3. The dog trusted his master.

4. I have baked five potatoes for dinner.

5. The baked potatoes will be served with sour cream.

6. The potatoes, served hot, quickly cooled.

7. Grandmother baked a ham for the family reunion.

8. The exhausted child was sleeping on his father's lap.

9. We have exhausted every source of income.

10. The partygoers, exhausted from an all-night fling, straggled towards their cars.

Use the answer key to check your work. Mark the results below. Then discuss any incorrect answers with your instructor.

No. Correct: . . . .   *No. Incorrect:* . . . .

● EXERCISE 41

Write a sentence of your own for each of the following words. Underline the subject and the verb in each sentence.

1. frightened   . . . .

. . . .

2. closed   . . . .

. . . .

3. sacrificed   . . . .

. . . .

4. whipped   . . . .

. . . .

5. loved   . . . .

. . . .

Show your work to your instructor. Mark your score below.

No. Correct: . . . .   *No. Incorrect:* . . . .

Irregular Verbs

The past participle of *irregular verbs* is unpredictable. There are no simple rules for making the past participle of irregular verbs. You have to know them from memory or look them up in a dictionary.

EXAMPLES

Root	Past Participle
grow	grown
lose	lost
do	done
hurt	hurt
break	broken
be	been

● EXERCISE 42

Write the past participle form of each of the following irregular verbs. (If you are not sure of the form, look up the verb in the dictionary.)

1. know   . . . .   4. put   . . . .

2. leave   . . . .   5. speak   . . . .

3. go   . . . .   6. hide   . . . .

7. drink . . . .   9. buy . . . .

8. tell . . . .   10. bring . . . .

Use the answer key to check your work. Mark the results below. Then discuss any incorrect answers with your instructor.

No. Correct: . . . .   *No. Incorrect:* . . . .

What is true about past participles of régular verbs in sentences is also true about past participles of irregular verbs.

By itself the past participle never functions as a verb in a sentence.

EXAMPLES

         s   v
<u>Grown</u> children leave home.

         s   v
The puppy, <u>lost</u> for hours, finally found its way home.

But the past participle can be a verb if it has a helping verb in front of it.

EXAMPLES

         s   v
Tony <u>has grown</u> three inches in one year.

                s   v
Those dimes <u>were lost</u> by my brother.

The past participle of *most* irregular verbs is different from the past tense.

EXAMPLES

Root	Past Tense	Past Participle
do	did	done
go	went	gone
ride	rode	ridden
eat	ate	eaten
sing	sang	sung
see	saw	seen

The past tense is a verb by itself but the past participle needs a helping verb in front of it to function as a verb.

EXAMPLES

Rick did his work.

He has done his work.

They saw that movie five times.

They have seen that movie five times.

● EXERCISE 43

Underline the subject and the verb in each of the following sentences. Put parentheses around any past participle that is not part of a verb phrase. (The first three items are examples.)

1. We ate at a restaurant last Saturday.

2. They have eaten at a restaurant every Saturday this month.

3. My car, (eaten) away with rust, is falling apart.

4. The choir sang gospel music.

5. The choir has sung together for many years.

6. Gospel music sung by a choir lifts your spirit.

7. The candidate for Congress spoke on foreign policy.

8. I have spoken to the landlord about the plumbing.

9. Some people have no respect for the spoken word.

10. A word spoken in jest may return to haunt you.

Use the answer key to check your work. Mark the results below. Then discuss any incorrect answers with your instructor.

No. Correct: . . . .   *No. Incorrect:* . . . .

● EXERCISE 44

Write a sentence of your own for each of the following words.

1. did   ....

   ....

2. done   ....

   ....

3. went   ....

   ....

4. gone   ....

   ....

5. saw   ....

   ....

6. seen   ....

   ....

Show your work to your instructor. Mark your score below.

No. Correct: ....   *No. Incorrect:* ....

The past participle of *some* irregular verbs is the same as the past tense.

EXAMPLES

Root	Past Tense	Past Participle
spend	spent	spent
win	won	won
have	had	had
cost	cost	cost
hurt	hurt	hurt

The past tense is a verb by itself, but the past participle must have a helping verb in front of it to be a verb.

EXAMPLES

    s   v

Jenny lost her marbles   (past tense)

     s   v

Jenny *has* lost her marbles.   (past participle)

       s   v

Hurt feelings are no laughing matter.   (past participle)

   s   v

Ron *has* hurt his knee.   (past participle)

    s   v

Bonnie hurt her elbow.   (past tense)

● EXERCISE 45

Underline the subject and the verb in each of the following sentences. Put parentheses around any past participle that is not part of a verb phrase. (The first three items are examples.)

1. Diane spent all her money on food.

2. Claude has spent the night with a friend.

3. Money (spent) on foolishness is a waste.

4. The game was won by the home team.

5. Won in August, the pennant race was without excitement in September.

6. Somebody from Indiana won a million dollars in the lottery.

7. Her team has won every game this year.

8. Cars made in Japan are as good as American cars.

9. Richard made an error in balancing his checkbook.

10. The Beatles have not made a new record together for years.

Use the answer key to check your work. Mark the results below. Then discuss any incorrect answers with your instructor.

No. Correct: . . . .   *No. Incorrect:* . . . .

● EXERCISE 46

Write a sentence of your own for each óf the following words.

1. cost ....

....

2. thought ....

....

3. stood ....

....

4. shot ....

....

5. hit ....

....

Show your work to your instructor. Mark your score below.

No. Correct: ....   *No. Incorrect:* ....

● EXERCISE 47: REVIEW

Underline the subject and the verb in each of the following sentences. Mark *s* above the subject and *v* above the verb.

1. The museums provide something for everyone.

2. The runner ran around third base.

3. Trying to let in some fresh air, Doris opened a window.

4. The air outside was worse than the air inside.

5. Annie yielded to Jack's sweet talk.

6. Unemployment is getting worse.

7. Partying is fun.

8. Sue wants to quit her job.

9. Bert stumbled through the lobby of the union.

10. The excited horse threw its rider.

11. Have they started the game yet?

12. The hunter on safari killed two lions.

13. I haven't got any money for the movie.

14. There are two new theaters in town.

15. I enjoy going to the movies.

16. The pitcher pitched a wild pitch.

17. That wild pitch of his cost him the game.

18. The following students should report to the dean's office.

19. I have been following tennis for years.

20. This sentence is the last one in this exercise.

Use the answer key to check your work. Mark the results below. Then discuss any incorrect answers with your instructor.

No. Correct: . . . .   *No. Incorrect:* . . . .

You have completed *Section Two*, Verb Recognition. Now go back to page 8 and complete *Section One*, Sentence Fundamentals.

SECTION THREE

Sentence Elements

The two major facts you need to know about sentences are:

1. Every sentence has a main clause.
2. Every clause has a subject and a verb.

A complete sentence may consist of a main clause with only two words in it.

EXAMPLES

   s   v
Birds fly.

   s   v
Ted won.

These are correct sentences, for each one has a main clause that has a subject and a verb.

Most sentences, however, have more than two words.

EXAMPLES

        s   v
Many birds fly south in the winter.

                      S   V

Many birds, driven by some mysterious instinct, fly thousands
of miles to return to the area where they were born.

      S   V

Ted won the prize.

      S   V

Ted, who practiced for six months, won a prize for public
speaking.

Notice that the key elements of the sentence, the subject and the verb,
stay the same, but any number of other elements can be added. It is
these other elements that this section is about.

● EXERCISE 48

If a group of words is a correct sentence, capitalize the first word and put a
period at the end. If a group of words is not a sentence, write *fragment* after
the last word.

1. the end of the race was marked by great confusion

2. frightened by the sound of an owl in the cemetery

3. the faucet drips

4. dripping faucet in the bathroom

5. at first

6. he laughs

7. which is in England

8. the Isle of Wight, which is in England, has an excellent climate

9. when the Spanish first landed in the New World

10. they thought that they were in India

Use the answer key to check your work. Mark the results below. Then discuss
any incorrect answers with your instructor.

No. Correct: . . . .   *No. Incorrect:* . . . .

The terms this section will cover are:

> Direct and indirect objects.
>
> One-word modifiers.
>
> Phrase modifiers.
>
> Subordinate-clause modifiers.

A subordinate clause, in addition to having a subject and a verb, may also have objects, one-word modifiers, and phrase modifiers.

A phrase also may have objects and one-word modifiers.

The main reason for dealing with the different types of objects and modifiers is so that you can tell them apart from *subjects, verbs,* and *main clauses.* When you can do this, you can understand how the different types of sentences are put together.

DIRECT OBJECTS AND INDIRECT OBJECTS

1. *Every* verb has a subject.
2. *Some* verbs have a direct object.
3. A *few* verbs have both a direct object and an indirect object.

    EXAMPLES

           s   v
    1. The telephone rang. (*Rang* has no direct or indirect object.)

           s   v
        Albert died after a brief illness. (*Died* has no direct or indirect object.)

              s   v   do
    2. The secretary found a wallet. (*Found* has a direct object, *wallet.*)

           s   v   do
        Sally told the truth. (*Told* has a direct object, *truth.*)

           s   v   io   do
    3. Sally told her mother the truth. (Here *told* has both a direct object, *truth*, and an indirect object, *mother.*)

            s   v io   do
        Bonnie gave Joe a kiss. (*Gave* has both a direct object, *kiss*, and an indirect object, *Joe.*)

NOTE: In everyday usage the word *object* means the same as the word *thing*. But in grammar an object can be a *person*, a *place*, an *idea*, or a *quality* as well as a thing.

EXAMPLES

    v   do
William threw the <u>ball</u>. (The object is a *thing*.)

    v do
The ball hit <u>Robert</u>. (The object is a *person*.)

     v   do
Columbus discovered <u>America</u>. (The object is a *place*.)

      v   do
The revolutionists defended <u>freedom</u>. (The object is an *idea*.)

     v do
Some people lack <u>patience</u>. (The object is a *quality*.)

The direct object is connected directly *in meaning* with the verb. If a word is not connected with the verb in meaning, it is not a direct object.

EXAMPLES

    v   do
1. John <u>ran</u> the race. (*Race* is directly connected in meaning with *ran*. Therefore *race* is a direct object.)

    v
John <u>ran</u> into the wall. (In meaning, *wall* is connected with *into* not with *ran*. Therefore *wall* is not a direct object.)

     v   do
2. The roof is <u>leaking</u> <u>water</u>. (*Water* is the direct object of the verb.)

    v
Water is <u>leaking</u> from the faucet. (*Faucet* is not the direct object of the verb.)

● EXERCISE 49

The verbs are already marked in the following sentences. If the verb has a *direct object*, underline it. (Four of the verbs do *not* have a direct object.)

    v
1. The children <u>are playing</u> baseball.

    v
2. The children <u>are playing</u> in the street.

3. The soldier <u>lost</u> his rifle.
   v

4. The rain <u>fell</u> rapidly.
   v

5. Love <u>overcomes</u> selfishness.
   v

6. Ed <u>threw</u> up on the sidewalk.
   v

7. Some Russians <u>visited</u> Cincinnati.
   v

8. A snake <u>bit</u> the baby.
   v

9. Donna <u>is looking</u> under the bed for her watch.
   v

10. The explosion <u>knocked</u> Daniel against the wall.
    v

Use the answer key to check your work. Mark the results below. Then discuss any incorrect answers with your instructor.

No. Correct: . . . .   *No. Incorrect:* . . . .

___

An indirect object *receives* the direct object. Therefore in order to have an indirect object you must have a direct object.

> *EXAMPLES*
>
>   v   io   do
> The dean sent me a letter.
>
>   v   io   do
> The juniors gave the seniors a party.

● EXERCISE 50

The verbs are already marked in the following sentences. Mark *io* above the indirect object and *do* above the direct object. (The first item is an example.)

          v   io   do
1. The bankers <u>gave</u> Goodwill a large donation.

v
2. The cocktails <u>gave</u> Sharon a headache.

v
3. George <u>threw</u> me the newspaper.

v
4. My uncle <u>has written</u> the newspaper an angry letter.

v
5. Hitler <u>gave</u> patriotism a bad name.

Use the answer key to check your work. Mark the results below. Then discuss
any incorrect answers with your instructor.

No. Correct: . . . .   *No. Incorrect:* . . . .

A subject is not always the word right in front of the verb. And so, too,
the direct object or indirect object is not always the word right *after*
the verb.

> *EXAMPLES*
>
>   s   v   do
> 1. The <u>drunk</u> <u>was singing</u> a song.
>
>   s   v
> The <u>drunk</u> on the corner <u>was singing</u> his favorite sentimental
> do
> <u>song</u>.
>
>   s   v
> The <u>drunk</u> on the corner under the streetlight <u>was singing</u>, over
>   do
> and over and over again, his favorite sentimental <u>song</u>.
>
>   s   v   io   do
> 2. All the <u>stores</u> <u>sent</u> my sister bills.
>
>   s   v
> All the <u>stores</u> from the most expensive shopping area <u>sent</u> my
>   io   do
> carefree and thriftless <u>sister</u> huge and unpayable <u>bills</u>.

Although other words may come in between, the usual word order is:

1. subject   2. verb   3. indirect object   4. direct object.

REMINDER: Not every sentence has a direct object or indirect
object.

● EXERCISE 51

In the following sentences, the subject, the verb, the indirect object (if there is one), and the direct object are underlined. Mark *s* above the subject, *v* above the verb, *io* above the indirect object, and *do* above the direct object.

1. The children were eating their favorite chocolate candy.

2. Teenagers often give their parents a hard time.

3. The aging champion conquered, at the last moment, the dangerous young challenger.

4. A lover, impatient and reckless, was climbing a high, slippery, ivy-covered, spike-topped wall.

5. The man washing dishes gave the pots another scrubbing.

Use the answer key to check your work. Mark the results below. Then discuss any incorrect answers with your instructor.

No. Correct: . . . .   *No. Incorrect:* . . . .

● EXERCISE 52

Write three sentences of your own containing a direct object. Use the following words as verbs in your sentences.

1. broke   . . . .

. . . .

2. cleaned   . . . .

. . . .

3. made   . . . .

. . . .

Write two sentences of your own containing an indirect object as well as a direct object. Use the following words as the verbs in your sentences.

1. gave   . . . .

    . . . .

2. sent   . . . .

    . . . .

Show your work to your instructor. Mark your score below.

No. Correct: . . . .   *No. Incorrect:* . . . .

COMPOUNT SUBJECTS, VERBS, DIRECT OBJECTS, AND INDIRECT OBJECTS

The conjunction *and* sometimes joins two main clauses in order to make a compound sentence.

EXAMPLE

$$\text{s} \qquad \text{v} \qquad\qquad\qquad \text{s} \qquad \text{v}$$

The lamp crashed to the floor | and | the baby screamed.

But at other times the conjunction *and* joins two subjects, two verbs, two direct objects, or two indirect objects.

EXAMPLES

	s s
Compound Subject:	Betty and her sister live at home.

	v v
Compound Verb:	He eats and drinks a lot.

	v v
	He ate a bucket of chicken and drank a bottle of wine.

NOTE: *And* joins the words *ate* and *drank*, not *chicken* and *drank*.

	do do
Compound Direct Object:	The dog has ticks and fleas.

	io io
Compound Indirect Object:	Grandpa gave Don and Rose some books.

● EXERCISE 53

In the following sentences put a box around the word *and*. Underline the two words that *and* joins together. Mark the appropriate letters — *s, v, do,* or *io* — above both words of the compound.

1. That singer has had great success and fame.

2. Yesterday Shawn and Ken gave their cousin a surprise birthday party.

3. Many people live and die in the same city.

4. Jane cut and sewed a skirt and a blouse.

5. The dude in handcuffs was telling the cop and the reporters a totally incredible story.

6. Joe and I have known each other for years.

7. The host of the party cut the cake and passed it around.

8. The sailor brought his little brother a statue and a sword from Japan.

Use the answer key to check your work. Mark the results below. Then discuss any incorrect answers with your instructor.

No. Correct: . . . .   *No. Incorrect:* . . . .

MODIFIERS

Everything in a sentence that is not a subject, a verb, a direct object, or an indirect object is a modifier.

Modifiers describe or give additional information or details about subjects, verbs, objects, or other modifiers.

There are three types of modifiers:

1.   One-word modifiers.

EXAMPLES

<pre>
        m   s   m   v   m   do
The delighted crowd loudly cheered the proud champion.
</pre>

NOTE: The words *the*, *a* and *an* are considered modifiers; but since they are so common, they are not marked in the examples or the exercises.

2.   Phrase modifiers.

EXAMPLES

<pre>
        m   s   v   do   m
Running to catch a bus, Holly dropped her purse on the sidewalk.
</pre>

3.   Subordinate clause modifiers.

EXAMPLES

<pre>
      s   m   v   m
The man that lived next door moved because the rent went
up.
</pre>

Modifiers can come *before*, *after*, or *between* any of the other sentence elements. *There can be any number of modifiers in a sentence.*

One-Word Modifiers

A one-word modifier usually comes right before the word it modifies.

In the following examples, a modifier of a subject is marked *ms*, a modifier of a verb is marked *mv*, a modifier of a direct object is marked *mdo*, and a modifier of another modifier is marked *mm*.

EXAMPLES

<pre>
  ms   s   v mm mdo   do
The blue shirt has very fine stitches.

    s   mv   v
The truck suddenly stopped.

  ms   s   v   mdo   do
The excited cat found a stinking fish.
</pre>

A modifier of a verb may come anywhere in a sentence.

EXAMPLES

    mv   **v**
Suddenly the truck stopped.

        mv   **v**
The truck suddenly stopped.

        v   **mv**
The truck stopped suddenly.

Modifiers of verbs answer the questions:

  1. When?

      EXAMPLES: now, yesterday, soon

  2. Where?

      EXAMPLES: here, there, everywhere

  3. How?

      EXAMPLES: quickly, easily, angrily

● EXERCISE 54

In the following sentences, the subject, verb, and direct object are marked.
Mark the modifiers *ms, mv, mdo* or *mm*. (The first item is an example.)

        ms   **s**   **mv**   **v**   **mdo do**
1. The disappointed politician finally conceded his defeat.

        s   **v**   **do**
2. The old man crossed the busy street very slowly.

           s   **v**   **do**
3. Soon the whole neighborhood will know the gory details.

         s   **v**   **do**
4. Whispering winds softly caressed the drowsy lovers.

        s   **v**   **do**
5. The movers, hot and tired, are unloading the final pieces of furniture now.

Use the answer key to check your work. Mark the results below. Then discuss
any incorrect answers with your instructor.

No. Correct: . . . .   *No. Incorrect: . . . .*

Phrase Modifiers

A phrase is any group of words that *does not have* both a subject and a verb.

Three types of phrases function as modifiers:

1. Prepositional phrases

    EXAMPLES

    on the table

    because of the heavy rain

    in spite of your kindness

2. Participial phrases

    EXAMPLES

    swinging wildly

    dropping his pants

    cornered by a mob

3. Infinitive phrases

    EXAMPLES

    to buy a new shirt

    to find an answer

Prepositional Phrase Modifiers

A prepositional phrase is a group of words that begins with a *preposition* and ends with the *object* of the preposition.

A preposition always has an object. Therefore a prepositional phrase always has at least two words. But any number of modifiers can come in between the preposition and its object.

EXAMPLES

<u>in</u> the <u>bedroom</u>

op

<u>next to</u> the <u>lady</u>

op

<u>with</u> the large blue <u>purse</u>

op

<u>because of</u> his difficult <u>boss</u>

Here are three lists of some common prepositions.

ONE-WORD PREPOSITIONS

at	about	across
by	after	against
for	among	around
from	before	behind
in	below	beside
of	down	between
on	into	during
to	over	except
with	under	through
	upon	without

TWO-WORD PREPOSITIONS

ahead of	except for	next to
because of	inside of	out of
due to	instead of	up to

THREE-WORD PREPOSITIONS

by means of	in spite of
in addition to	on account of
in back of	on top of

● EXERCISE 55

In the following prepositional phrases, put one line under the *preposition* and put two lines under the *object of the preposition*.

1. by the table

2. with her sister

3. except for the carpenter

4. between them

5. behind all the dusty furniture

6. because of the rain

7. without his best and most trusted friend

8. from the very first moment

9. by due process

10. in addition to the long-necked giraffes

Use the answer key to check your work. Mark the results below. Then discuss any incorrect answers with your instructor.

No. Correct: . . . .   *No. Incorrect:* . . . .

A prepositional phrase may modify a subject, a verb, and any kind of object, even the object of another preposition.

A prepositional phrase usually comes *after* the word it modifies.

> *EXAMPLES*
>
> NOTE: A prepositional phrase that modifies the object of another preposition is marked *mop*.
>
> | | s | ms | mop | v | mv |
> The book <u>by the lamp</u> <u>on the table</u> belongs <u>to me.</u>
>
> | | v | mv |
> The game was cancelled <u>due to rain.</u>
>
> | | do | mdo |
> I injured the bottom <u>of my foot.</u>

But a prepositional phrase that modifies a verb may come at the beginning of the sentence or at the end, as well as right next to the verb.

> *EXAMPLES*
>
> <u>In spite of the rain</u> the plane arrived on time.
>
> The plane, <u>in spite of the rain,</u> arrived on time.
>
> The plane arrived, <u>in spite of the rain,</u> on time.
>
> The plane arrived on time <u>in spite of the rain.</u>

Prepositional phrases that modify verbs answer the questions:

1. When?

    EXAMPLES:

    on Tuesday

    after the show

2. Where?

    EXAMPLES:

    in the kitchen

    next to the bar

3. How?

    EXAMPLES:

    with a sudden jerk

    by means of his sharp wits

4. Why?

    EXAMPLES:

    because of the accident

    due to inflation

● EXERCISE 56

Underline all the prepositional phrases in the following sentences. (The first item is an example.)

1. Greg was looking <u>for a job</u> <u>at the shopping center</u>.

2. In late August Jerry was wearing a heavy coat in spite of the heat.

3. The woman ahead of me in line was complaining about the air conditioner over our heads.

4. The tips of his two front teeth were broken in a fight with some kids from another school.

5.   On Friday night Mary left her new gloves on the table in the kitchen of the apartment of her closest friend.

Use the answer key to check your work. Mark the results below. Then discuss any incorrect answers with your instructor.

No. Correct: . . . .   *No. Incorrect:* . . . .

• EXERCISE 57

Write three prepositional phrases of your own, then use each one in a sentence.

   EXAMPLE: *Prepositional Phrase:*   in the corner
                     Sentence: The wastebasket is in the corner.

1. *Prepositional Phrase:*   . . . .

   Sentence: . . . .

                            . . . .

2. *Prepositional Phrase:*   . . . .

   Sentence: . . . .

                            . . . .

3. *Prepositional Phrase:*   . . . .

   Sentence: . . . .

                            . . . .

Show your work to your instructor. Mark your score below.

No. Correct: . . . .   *No. Incorrect:* . . . .

Participial Phrase Modifiers

A participial phrase consists of a participle and any objects and modifiers that go with the participle.

   EXAMPLES

   (The participle is underlined.)

              io   do
   <u>giving</u> the teacher a funny look

> **m**
> running swiftly

> **m**   **m**
> dressed primly and properly

> **m**
> written hastily

A participial phrase may even contain a prepositional phrase as a modifier.

> *EXAMPLES*
>
> shining in the sky
>
> blasted by dynamite

A participial phrase is used as a modifier of a subject or an object.

> *EXAMPLES*
>
> **s**
> Running swiftly, Jack crossed the finish line first.
>
> **s**
> The star, shining in the sky, looked lonely.
>
> **do**
> Sue saw Albert giving the teacher a funny look.
>
> **op**
> A dirty cat brushed against a lady dressed primly and properly.
>
> **s**
> The letter, written hastily, was impossible to read.

● EXERCISE 58

Underline the participial phrases in the following sentences. (Item 1 is an example.)

1. The mountain, blasted by dynamite, was turned into a molehill.

2. I saw a bee flying from flower to flower.

3. Excited by catnip, the cat wriggled and purred.

4. Sensitive ears hate songs sung out of tune.

5. The fish, stinking to high heaven, gave him a headache.

Use the answer key to check your work. Mark the results below. Then discuss any incorrect answers with your instructor.

No. Correct: . . . .   *No. Incorrect: . . . .*

● EXERCISE 59

Write a participial phrase of your own using each of the following participles. Then use each of your phrases as a *modifier* of a subject or an object in a sentence.

   EXAMPLE:

   looking   *Participial Phrase:*   looking for an exit
              Sentence: Looking for an exit, John wandered
                                       through the huge department store.

1. dripping   *Participial Phrase:*   . . . .

               Sentence: . . . .

                                        . . . .

2. twisted   *Participial Phrase:*   . . . .

               Sentence: . . . .

                                        . . . .

3. bouncing   *Participial Phrase:*   . . . .

               Sentence: . . . .

                                        . . . .

4. stung   *Participial Phrase:*   . . . .

               Sentence: . . . .

                                        . . . .

5. broken   *Participial Phrase:*   . . . .

               Sentence: . . . .

                                        . . . .

Show your work to your instructor. Mark your score below.

No. Correct: . . . .   *No. Incorrect: . . . .*

Infinitive Phrase Modifiers

An infinitive phrase consists of an infinitive and any objects and modifiers that go with the infinitive.

> *EXAMPLES*
>
> (The infinitive is underlined.)
>
> <u>to tell</u> the truth
>
> <u>to conquer</u> the world
>
> <u>to float</u> gently in the breeze

An infinitive phrase can be used as a modifier.

> *EXAMPLES*
>
> <u>To tell the truth</u>, I don't like television.
>
> Gerald has a plan <u>to conquer the world</u>.

● EXERCISE 60

Underline the infinitive phrases in the following sentences. (Item 1 is an example.)

1. Her favorite groups are the Temptations, the Beach Boys, and the Jackson Five, <u>to mention just a few</u>.

2. His dream to float gently in the breeze was unreal.

3. I have a job to do in the morning.

4. You must drink a lot of coffee to drive from Chicago to New York in one day.

5. To be honest, I don't know the answer.

Use the answer key to check your work. Mark the results below. Then discuss any incorrect answers with your instructor.

No. Correct: . . . .   *No. Incorrect:* . . . .

● EXERCISE 61

Write an infinitive phrase of your own using each of the following infinitives. Then use each of your phrases in a sentence.

EXAMPLE

to finish   *Infinitive Phrase:*   to finish in first place

                   Sentence: You must try your hardest to finish in first place.

1. to go   *Infinitive Phrase:*   ....

              Sentence: ....

                            ....

2. to have   *Infinitive Phrase:*   ....

              Sentence: ....

                            ....

3. to live   *Infinitive Phrase:*   ....

              Sentence: ....

                            ....

Show your work to your instructor. Mark your score below.

No. Correct: ....   *No. Incorrect:* ....

Subordinate Clause Modifiers

Subordinate clauses function in two ways as modifiers:

   1. Modifiers of *verbs.*

      EXAMPLES

                                              v

      <u>Because the storm destroyed the crops</u>, the farmer had no income.

                v

      Randy took the clothes off the line <u>before the rain started.</u>

2. Modifiers of *subjects* or *objects*.

EXAMPLES

 s
The new record <u>that I want</u> costs seven dollars.

                                          o
The judge released the prisoner <u>who had been wrongfully</u>
<u>arrested.</u>

Review: Main Clauses and Subordinate Clauses

A clause is a group of words with both a subject and a verb.

A subordinate clause, therefore, just like a main clause, *always* has a subject and a verb in it. (A subordinate clause may also contain objects and modifiers just like a main clause.) The only difference between a main clause and a subordinate clause is that a subordinate clause begins with an extra word, a *subordinate conjunction.*

EXAMPLES

Main Clauses	*Subordinate Clauses* (The subordinate conjunction is underlined.)
s v The rain started.	s v <u>before</u> the rain started
s v The storm destroyed the crops.	s v <u>because</u> the storm destroyed the crops
s v I want.	s v <u>that</u> I want

Because of the subordinate conjunction, a subordinate clause is only a fragment of a sentence. But a main clause is a sentence by itself.

● EXERCISE 62

Mark *s* above the subject and *v* above the verb in the following clauses. If the clause is a *subordinate clause*, underline the subordinate conjunction at the beginning. If the clause is a *main clause*, capitalize the first word and put a period at the end. (Items 1 and 2 are examples.)

      T̸/ s   v
1. /the snow started to fall⊙

           s   v
2. <u>when</u> the snow started to fall

3. she is his boss

4. although she is his boss

5. I lost the watch

6. which I inherited from my grandfather

7. as the car pulled out of the driveway

8. it hit a bump

9. the senator met his wife

10. while they were in law school together

Use the answer key to check your work. Mark the results below. Then discuss any incorrect answers with your instructor.

No. Correct: . . . .   *No. Incorrect:* . . . .

Subordinate Clauses as Modifiers of Verbs

A subordinate clause that modifies a verb always begins with a subordinate conjunction such as these:

SUBORDINATE CONJUNCTIONS

after	though	as if
although	unless	as long as
as	until	even though
because	when	in order that
before	whenever	so that
if	where	
since	wherever	
than	while	

(There are others, but these are the most common ones.)

Sometimes it is hard to see how a subordinate clause modifies the verb. But like other modifiers of verbs, many subordinate clauses answer the questions: *When? Where?* or *Why?*

EXAMPLES

1. *When?*   Randy <u>took</u> the clothes off the line <u>before the</u>
   <u>rain started</u>.

   (V above "took")

2. *Where?*   <u>Wherever you go</u>, I <u>will follow</u> you.

   (V above "will follow")

3. *Why?*   <u>Because the storm destroyed the crops</u>, the

   farmer <u>had</u> no income.

   (V above "had")

Some subordinate clauses give a *condition* under which the main clause operates.

EXAMPLES

<u>If it is too cold</u>, the swimming party will be called off.

The concert will not continue, <u>unless the members of the</u>
<u>audience return to their seats</u>.

He will stay <u>as long as she wants him</u>.

A subordinate clause that modifies a verb may come either *before* or *after* the main clause.

EXAMPLES

<u>When the lights went out</u>, Doreen screamed.

Doreen screamed <u>when the lights went out</u>.

<u>Because the lawyer was not prepared</u>, John lost his case.

John lost his case <u>because the lawyer was not prepared</u>.

<u>If Germany had won World War II</u>, we might all be speaking
   German today.

We might all be speaking German today, <u>if Germany had won</u>
   <u>World War II</u>.

● EXERCISE 63

Underline the whole subordinate clause in the following sentences. Put a box around the subordinate conjunction at the beginning of the subordinate clause. (Item 1 is an example.)

1. ☐When☐ Sonny gets blue, her eyes get grey and cloudy.

2. Carefully they counted all the votes, although everyone already knew the result.

3. The captain ordered the firemen to let the fire burn because the walls were weakened and dangerous.

4. If the next sentence has two subordinate clauses in it, then you should underline both of them.

5. Because he had no money for the bus, Greg was walking in the rain to the restaurant where he worked.

Use the answer key to check your work. Mark the results below. Then discuss any incorrect answers with your instructor.

No. Correct: . . . .   *No. Incorrect:* . . . .

● EXERCISE 64

Write a subordinate clause of your own using each of the following subordinate conjunctions. Then use each of your subordinate clauses in a sentence.

EXAMPLE

since	*Subordinate Clause:*	since Pauline left town
	Sentence:	Everything has been quiet since Pauline left town.

1. when   *Subordinate Clause:*   . . . .

              Sentence: . . . .

                       . . . .

2. because   *Subordinate Clause:*   . . . .

              Sentence: . . . .

                       . . . .

3. if   *Subordinate Clause:*   . . . .

              Sentence: . . . .

                       . . . .

4. wherever *Subordinate Clause:* . . . .

                  Sentence: . . . .

                                     . . . .

5. although *Subordinate Clause:* . . . .

                  Sentence: . . . .

                                       . . . .

Show your work to your instructor. Mark your score below.

No. Correct: . . . .   *No. Incorrect:* . . . .

___

Subordinate Clauses as Modifiers of Subjects or Objects

A subordinate clause that is a modifier of a subject or an object begins with one of these words:

```
┌────────────────────────────────┐
│   that      who        which   │
│             whose              │
└────────────────────────────────┘
```

This kind of subordinate clause comes right *after* the word it modifies.

EXAMPLES

         s

The <u>man</u> that usually fixes my car was sick today.

            do

Anne met a <u>girl</u> who was a schoolmate of hers.

            io

Steve gave <u>Claudia</u>, whose father is rich, an engagement ring.

                  op

They took a drive to <u>Bardstown</u>, which is in Kentucky.

The word that signals the beginning of this kind of subordinate clause sometimes is also the subject of the subordinate clause. Sometimes another word is the subject.

EXAMPLES

           s   v

The man <u>that usually fixes my car</u> was sick today.

s   v

The man that I take my car to was sick today.

• EXERCISE 65

Underline the subordinate clauses in the following sentences. Put two lines under the word the subordinate clause modifies. (The first item is an example.)

1. Yesterday Donald gave my girl friend a warm hello that was much too friendly.

2. The lady who was crying in her beer had lost a winning ticket in the lottery.

3. Nobody would help the traveller whose car ran out of gas.

4. The red shoes, which Lisa bought just last week, are already falling apart.

5. A clever con artist who gains his victims' trust can easily cheat them out of their possessions.

Use the answer key to check your work. Mark the results below. Then discuss any incorrect answers with your instructor.

No. Correct: . . . .   *No. Incorrect:* . . . .

• EXERCISE 66

Finish the subordinate clauses in the following sentences with words of your own.

1. The book that . . . . is available at the campus bookstore.

2. Saul knows a lady who . . . .

3. Our plans for a picnic were ruined by the hail that. . . . .

    . . . .

4. The clerk who . . . . is on vacation.

5. Cincinnati, which . . . . ,
    has an exciting riverfront area.

Show your work to your instructor. Mark your score below.

No. Correct: . . . .   *No. Incorrect:* . . . .

A Special Case: Comparisons

Subordinate clauses are sometimes used to make comparisons. In this case, the subordinate clause modifies another modifier.

EXAMPLES

m
We all can speak more quickly <u>than we can write</u>.

m
The guests left as soon <u>as dinner was finished</u>.

The subordinate conjunctions used in making comparisons are:

as	than

● EXERCISE 67

Underline the subordinate clauses in the following sentences.

1. You are welcome to visit as often as you want to.

2. Delighted by Jim's eagerness, Anne made her move sooner than she had planned.

Use the answer key to check your work. Mark the results below. Then discuss any incorrect answers with your instructor.

No. Correct: . . . .   *No. Incorrect:* . . . .

DISTINGUISHING BETWEEN MAIN CLAUSES AND SUBORDINATE CLAUSES AND PHRASES

A main clause has a subject and a verb and can stand alone as a sentence.

> A subordinate clause also has a subject and a verb but cannot stand alone as a sentence, because it begins with a subordinate conjunction.
>
> A phrase does not have a subject and a verb and therefore cannot stand alone as a sentence.

From these three statements it is clear that one of the keys to distinguishing between main clauses, subordinate clauses, and phrases is recognizing whether or not a group of words has a subject and a verb. For this reason, it is useful here to review the material on subjects and verbs covered in *Section Two* of this book.

Review: Verb Recognition

1. Meaning.

    A verb means either an action or condition (state of being).

Action Verbs	*Condition (State of Being) Verbs*
sing	is
run	were
think	seem

    Many words can be verbs but these same words are not always verbs.

    v
    I <u>love</u> you.

    s
    Our <u>love</u> is beautiful.

    v
    You <u>smoke</u> too much.

    s
    <u>Smoke</u> filled the room.

2. Subject/verb relation.

    Every verb has a subject.

    s   v
    The <u>clock</u> <u>ticks</u> constantly.

    s   v
    The <u>color</u> of the rose <u>was</u> red.

3. Position.

    A verb usually comes *after* its subject.

    s   v
    The <u>boy</u> <u>tripped</u> on a rock.

EXCEPTIONS: In sentences beginning *there is, there are* or *here is, here are* and in *questions*, the verb comes *before* the subject.

$$\overset{\text{v}}{\text{are}} \quad \overset{\text{s}}{\text{children}}$$

There are three children in the yard.

$$\overset{\text{v}}{\text{Is}} \quad \overset{\text{s}}{\text{Calvin}}$$

Is Calvin your brother?

Any number of words can come in between a subject and a verb.

$$\overset{\text{s}}{\text{boy}} \qquad\qquad\qquad\qquad \overset{\text{v}}{\text{tripped}}$$

The boy, running across the parking lot, tripped on a rock.

4. Form.

A verb can change form in many ways.

jump:

jump:		
jumps	am jumping	jumped
will jump	is jumping	has jumped
did jump	was jumping	have jumped
can jump	could be jumping	would have jumped

These are only some forms of the verb *jump*.

● EXERCISE 68: REVIEW

Underline the subject and the verb in the following sentences. Mark *s* above the subject and *v* above the verb.

1. Many sky-divers jump every weekend.

2. The jump from the plane broke the sky-diver's leg.

3. Richard jumped out of the way of the bicycle.

4. Here is the book on the psychology of personality.

5. Her old apartment depressed her.

6. Are your friends ready for action?

7. Sometimes tensions between husband and wife cause trouble for their children.

8. The cause of her excitement was her boy friend's return.

9. There are often problems to finding a subject and a verb.

10. Was the first answer the correct one?

Use the answer key to check your work. Mark the results below. Then discuss any incorrect answers with your instructor.

No. Correct: . . . .   *No. Incorrect:* . . . .

5. Time.

A verb tells the time of the action or condition of its subject.

The three basic times of verbs are the *present*, the *past*, and the *future*.

Present Tense	*Past Tense*	*Future Tense*
I <u>dance</u>.	I <u>danced</u>.	I <u>will dance</u>.
She <u>is</u> sorry.	She <u>was</u> sorry.	She <u>will be</u> sorry.

6. Verb phrases.

A verb may have more than one word to it; in this case the verb is a verb phrase.

A verb phrase consists of the *main verb* and one or more *helping verbs* in front of the main verb.

    will come   have been climbing   may have talked

When you are asked to find the verb in a sentence, be sure to find *the whole verb phrase.*

Sometimes verb phrases are interrupted by other words.

The sun <u>is</u> not <u>shining</u> today.

<u>Have</u> the neighbors in the next apartment <u>stopped</u> their noise?

7. Words that are always verbs.

You should know these lists of verbs by memory.

I.

am	do	has
is	does	have
are	did	had
was		
were		

The words in this first list can be verbs by themselves in sentences or they can be helping verbs.

I <u>am</u> ready.   She <u>does</u> her best.

I <u>am</u> leaving now.   She <u>does</u> love you.

II.	shall	would	may
	must	should	
		could	

The words in this second list are always helping verbs.

John <u>must behave</u> himself.

Mary <u>could win</u> the championship.

III.	will	can	might

The words in this third list are almost always helping verbs.

I <u>will go</u> first.

You <u>can follow</u> me.

We <u>might make</u> it.

(Here are some examples where these words are *not* verbs: free *will*; tin *can*; the *might* of God.)

8. Verbs and verbals.

Verbals look like verbs but by themselves they never function as verbs in sentences.

There are three kinds of verbals: *infinitives*, *gerunds*, and *participles*.

An *infinitive* is made of the word *to* and the root of the verb.

to dance   to think   to be

Infinitives never function as verbs in sentences.

A *gerund* is made by adding *ing* to the root of the verb.

talking   riding   grabbing

Gerunds function as subjects or objects but never as verbs.

s

<u>Swimming</u> is good exercise.

do

He should stop <u>talking</u>.

There are two kinds of participles: *present participles* and *past participles*.

The *present participle*, like the gerund, is made by adding *ing* to the root of the verb.

swaying   sliding   dripping

The *past participle* of *regular verbs*, like the past tense, is made by adding *d* or *ed* to the root of the verb.

smoked   created   returned

The *past participle* of *irregular verbs* is unpredictable. You must know them by memory or look them up in the dictionary.

grown   hurt   done

By themselves, *participles* function as modifiers of subjects or objects. Participles never function as verbs in sentences *unless* they have helping verbs in front of them.

           m
The <u>swaying</u> branches are graceful.

                v
The branches <u>are swaying</u> in the wind.

   m
<u>Smoked</u> salmon is expensive.

           v
Robert <u>has smoked</u> since the fourth grade.

  m
<u>Grown</u> children leave home.

        v
Tony <u>has grown</u> three inches in one year.

● EXERCISE 69 : REVIEW

===

Underline the subject and the verb in each of the following sentences. Mark *s* above the subject and *v* above the verb.

1.   The concert finally started after a two-hour delay.

2.   Is Jack your brother?

3.   A girl in a bikini was shopping in the grocery store.

4.   Take me to the river.

5.   There is a grease spot on your shirt.

6. He should not have pulled so hard on the door.

7. I surrender to your charms.

8. The surrender of the enemy ended the war.

9. In spite of the fog, the planes are arriving on time.

10. The movements of the sun and the moon are important influences on the weather.

11. The machinists have been thinking about going on strike.

12. At the end of this exercise you will certainly deserve a break.

13. Did Edison invent the electric light?

14. When will you put the chops in the oven?

15. To survive is the name of the game.

16. On Wednesday Rhoda caught Paul walking in the park with another girl.

17. Caught in the act of flirting with his best friend's fiancée, Louis could only smile.

18. Winning requires concentration and skill.

19. To avoid some broken glass, Earl suddenly jumped into the street.

20. Her singing could have broken a glass.

Use the answer key to check your work. Mark the results below. Then discuss any incorrect answers with your instructor.

No. Correct: . . . .   *No. Incorrect:* . . . .

DISTINGUISHING BETWEEN CLAUSES AND PHRASES

Every clause has a subject and a verb.

Every phrase *lacks* a subject and a verb.

If a group of words has a subject and a verb, then you know it is a clause. If a group of words does not have a subject and a verb, then you know it is a phrase.

> *EXAMPLES*
>
> on the car   (phrase)
>
>   s   v
> The tree fell on the car.   (clause)
>
> falling on the car   (phrase)
>
>   s   v
> while the tree <u>was falling</u> on the car   (clause)
>
> to fall on the car   (phrase)

● EXERCISE 70

Underline the subject and the verb in the following groups of words. If there is no subject and verb, write *phrase* next to the group. If there is a subject and a verb, write *clause* next to the group. (The first two items are examples.)

1. <u>John</u> <u>loves</u> Betty *clause.*

2. shouted by Danny *phrase*

3. down the street

4. since Gloria broke her leg

5. looking for the answer

6. to pay his debts

7. he was feeling happy

8. across the river

9. while the fans shouted encouragement

10. quickly jumping from tree to tree

Use the answer key to check your work. Mark the results below. Then discuss any incorrect answers with your instructor.

No. Correct: . . . .   *No. Incorrect:* . . . .

Some words can be used either as a preposition or as a subordinate conjunction. As a preposition the word begins a prepositional *phrase*. As a subordinate conjunction the word begins a subordinate *clause*.

> *EXAMPLES*
>
> <u>after</u> midnight   (phrase)
>
>   s   v
> <u>after</u> the clock struck midnight   (clause)
>
> <u>until</u> the last minute   (phrase)
>
>   s   v
> <u>until</u> the rain stops   (clause)

NOTE: *because of* is a preposition; *because* is a subordinate conjunction.

> *EXAMPLES*
>
> <u>because of</u> the war   (phrase)
>
>   s   v
> <u>because</u> the war disrupted society   (clause)

Again the key to distinguishing between a phrase and a clause is recognizing whether or not a group of words has a subject and a verb.

● EXERCISE 71

In the following groups of words, if there is no subject and verb, write *phrase* next to the group. If there is a subject and verb, underline them and write *clause* next to the group.

1. before they come

2. before supper

3. because of the broken dial on the TV set

4. because the term is over

5. since the start

Use the answer key to check your work. Mark the results below. Then discuss any incorrect answers with your instructor.

No. Correct: . . . .   *No. Incorrect: . . . .*

● EXERCISE 72

Write a phrase and a subordinate clause using each of the following words.

1. after   *Phrase:*   . . . .

               Subordinate Clause: . . . .

2. until   *Phrase:*   . . . .

               Subordinate Clause: . . . .

3. before   *Phrase:*   . . . .

               Subordinate Clause: . . . .

4. because   *Phrase:*   . . . .
    of
    because   *Subordinate Clause:*   . . . .

Show your work to your instructor. Mark your score below.

No. Correct: . . . .   *No. Incorrect:* . . . .

DISTINGUISHING BETWEEN MAIN CLAUSES AND SUBORDINATE CLAUSES

Both a main clause and a subordinate clause must have a subject and a verb. A subordinate clause, like a main clause, may also have a direct object, an indirect object, and any number of modifiers.

The *only difference* between a main clause and a subordinate clause is that a *subordinate clause begins with a subordinate conjunction.*

EXAMPLES

    s   v
We finished yesterday.   (main clause)

          s   v
<u>although</u> we finished yesterday   (subordinate clause)

   s   v   io   do
John gave Anne a juicy kiss.   (main clause)

        s   v   io   do
<u>when</u> John gave Anne a juicy kiss   (subordinate clause)

● EXERCISE 73

Underline the subject and the verb in each of the following clauses. Put a box around the subordinating conjunction at the beginning of each subordinate clause. Capitalize the first word and put a period at the end of each main clause. (Items 1 and 2 are examples.)

1. [since] he got out of the service

2. He got out of the service.

3. the ice has melted

4. because the smoke burned the firemen's eyes

5. John is a nice person

6. although I find him boring

7. that he bought

8. the desk belonged to her grandfather

9. if a group of words has a subject and a verb in it

10. it started a long time ago

Use the answer key to check your work. Mark the results below. Then discuss any incorrect answers with your instructor.

No. Correct: . . . .   *No. Incorrect:* . . . .

● EXERCISE 74

Write a paragraph about one of the following topics. Use sentences with a variety of phrases and clauses to show what you have learned from this section. (Make sure that each sentence has a main clause.)

Topics:

Your opinion of a movie you have seen recently.

Your opinion of a recent news item.

An important experience you have had as a college student.

Your paragraph should have:

1. A sentence at the beginning giving your controlling idea.
2. At least six sentences that develop your idea.
3. A concluding sentence.

· ·

· ·

· ·

· ·

· ·

· ·

· ·

· ·

· ·

· ·

· ·

· ·

· ·

· ·

· ·

· ·

· ·

· ·

Show your paragraph to your instructor.

You have now finished *Section Three*, Sentence Elements. Now go on to *Section Four*, Sentence Types.

SECTION FOUR

Sentence Types

Sentences can be classified by function or grammatical construction. According to function, there are three types:

1. Sentences that give information or opinions.
2. Sentences that ask questions.
3. Sentences that make commands.

According to grammatical construction, there are also three types:

1. Simple sentence.
2. Compound sentence.
3. Complex sentence.

This section will go into detail about the three grammatical types of sentences: simple, compound, and complex.

CLASSIFICATION OF GRAMMATICAL SENTENCE TYPES

A grammatical sentence type is defined according to the number and type of clauses and conjunctions it contains.

A *simple* sentence has *one main clause.*

A *compound* sentence has *two or more main clauses* which are most commonly joined by a coordinating conjunction.

A *complex* sentence has at least *one main clause and at least one subordinate clause.* Each subordinate clause begins with a *subordinate conjunction.*

SIMPLE SENTENCES

A simple sentence has *one main clause.* A main clause has a subject and a verb that go together. It may also have any number of objects, one-word modifiers, and phrase modifiers.

> *EXAMPLES*
>
>   s   v
> The people quarreled.
>
>   s
> The people down the street on the third floor of the red brick
>   v
> building quarreled loudly until four in the morning about
>
> their money problems.

These are both simple sentences because each one has only *one main clause.*

● EXERCISE 75

Underline the subjects and the verbs in the following simple sentences. Mark *s* above the subject and *v* above the verb.

1. He entered the house swiftly through a side door.

2. Deborah was eating a sandwich.

3. The excited dog smelled his master coming home.

4. The mail carrier talking to the dog spoke in a quiet tone in order to keep the animal calm.

5. The worker on top of the telephone pole saw a boy bicycling down the street straight toward an open manhole.

Use the answer key to check your work. Mark the results below. Then discuss any incorrect answers with your instructor.

No. Correct: . . . .   *No. Incorrect:* . . . .

● EXERCISE 76

Write two short simple sentences. Underline the subject and verb in each sentence.

1. . . . .

2. . . . .

Write two very long simple sentences. Underline the subject and verb in each sentence. Use as many one-word modifiers and phrase modifiers as you can, but do *not* use any subordinate clause modifiers.

1. . . . .

. . . .

. . . .

2. . . . .

. . . .

. . . .

Show your work to your instructor. Mark your score below.

No. Correct: . . . .   *No. Incorrect:* . . . .

Compound Subjects, Verbs, and Objects

A simple sentence can have a compound subject (more than one subject).

EXAMPLE

    s   s   s   s   s   s
Betty, Bob, Ted, Alice, Mary, and Joe are coming to the party
tonight.

A simple sentence can have a compound verb (more than one verb).

EXAMPLE

    v   v   v
Mary washed, patched, and painted the kitchen walls herself.

A simple sentence can have a compound object (more than one object).

EXAMPLE

     do   do   do   do   do
Father put meat, potatoes, onions, carrots, and beans in the
stew.

NOTE: All objects, including indirect objects and objects of prepositions, can be compounded.

A simple sentence can have all of these: compound subject, compound verb, compound object.

EXAMPLE

    s   s   s   v   v   do
Mother, Dad, and Aunt Laverne bought and prepared the food,
    do   do
drinks, and paper supplies for the picnic tomorrow.

● EXERCISE 77

Put a box around the word *and*. Then underline the compounds in the following sentences. Mark the appropriate letters — *s*, *v*, or *do* — above each word in
a compound. (The first two items are examples.)

    s   s   s
1. <u>Mark</u>, <u>Jane</u>, |and| her little <u>sister</u> went to the store.

       do   do
2. He plays <u>piano</u> |and| <u>flute</u>.

3. Marsha sang and danced all night.

4. He saw Sherry and Doug together at the movies.

5. He watched and waited with jealous eyes.

6. My dog and cat destroyed my purple shoes and scattered newspapers all around the room.

7. Bill and Bob fought John, Jack, and two other men.

8. The bartender and the customers broke four chairs and a table last night.

9. Ted loved his wife on Mondays and hated her on Saturdays.

10. She read scorn and malicious intent in his pretty green eyes.

Use the answer key to check your work. Mark the results below. Then discuss any incorrect answers with your instructor.

No. Correct: . . . .   *No. Incorrect:* . . . .

● EXERCISE 78

Write two sentences with compound subjects. Underline each subject.

1. . . . .

. . . .

2. . . . .

. . . .

Write two sentences with compound verbs. Underline each verb.

1. . . . .

. . . .

2. . . . .

. . . .

Write two sentences with compound objects. Underline each object.

1. . . . .

. . . .

2. ....

....

Write two sentences that have a combination of compound subjects, compound verbs, and compound objects.

1. ....

....

2. ....

....

Show your work to your instructor. Mark your score below.

No. Correct: ....   *No. Incorrect:* ....

Modifiers

A simple sentence can have any number of one-word modifiers or phrase modifiers.

> *EXAMPLE*
> (The phrase modifiers are underlined.)
>
>   m   m
> The tall young man <u>wearing a striped rugby shirt</u> sat <u>under the shady tree</u> <u>reading a sex manual</u>.

Review of Phrases

A phrase is a group of related words *without a subject and a verb.*

There are three types of phrases used as modifiers:

1. *Prepositional Phrase:*   a group of related words beginning with a preposition

   EXAMPLES

   <u>in</u> the store
   <u>behind</u> the table
   <u>next to</u> the toaster

2. *Participial Phrase:*   a group of related words beginning with a participle

EXAMPLES

<u>refusing</u> any help
<u>being</u> difficult to understand
<u>running</u> around madly
<u>dropped</u> on the table
<u>hung</u> in the closet

3. *Infinitive Phrase:*   a group of related words beginning with an infinitive

EXAMPLES

<u>to do</u> his best
<u>to begin</u> understanding
<u>to get</u> ahead

● EXERCISE 79

Underline each prepositional phrase, participial phrase, and infinitive phrase in the following sentences. (The first two items are examples.)

1. Jim walked calmly <u>into the room</u>.

2. <u>Carrying his baby in his arms</u>, Bob wandered <u>through the department store</u>.

3. Betty went to the store to buy a ten-speed bicycle.

4. Quickly Tom fixed the motorcycle for Glenn.

5. The crew across the street are filming a television show to be broadcast next spring.

6. There are two telephones on the desk in Barbara's office.

7. Irritated by Alice's wasting time, mother told her to finish washing the car right away.

8. Larry, pressed for time, drove across the country in just three days.

9. The men, working the bulldozer, woke me up.

10.   The birds are singing love songs filled with lilting melodies.

Use the answer key to check your work. Mark the results below. Then discuss any incorrect answers with your instructor.

No. Correct: . . . .   *No. Incorrect:* . . . .

● EXERCISE 80

Write two simple sentences that contain prepositional phrases. Underline the subject and the verb.

1.   . . . .

. . . .

2.   . . . .

. . . .

Write two simple sentences that contain participial phrases. Underline the subject and the verb.

1.   . . . .

. . . .

2.   . . . .

. . . .

Write two simple sentences that contain infinitive phrases. Underline the subject and the verb.

1.   . . . .

. . . .

2.   . . . .

. . . .

Show your work to your instructor. Mark your score below.

No. Correct: . . . .   *No. Incorrect:* . . . .

COMPOUND SENTENCES

A compound sentence is a sentence with two or more main clauses. There are two ways commonly used to connect the main clauses:

1. Use a coordinate conjunction.
2. Use a semicolon (;).

1. Use a Coordinate Conjunction

A coordinate conjunction is used to join two main clauses to make a compound sentence. The coordinate conjunctions are:

and	or	so
but	nor	yet
	for	

EXAMPLES

    S   V   V   S   V V

The trees are swaying in the wind [and] the sky has turned dark with clouds.

    S   V   S   V

Clarence is a Republican [but] his wife is a Democrat.

Punctuation

NOTE: Use a comma before a coordinate conjunction if the clauses it joins are long.

EXAMPLE

                   S   V

In the summertime people spend a lot of time on outdoor

               S   V

activities[,] but in the winter people mostly sit around indoors eating and watching television.

● EXERCISE 81

In the following compound sentences, underline the subject and the verb in each main clause. Put a box around the coordinate conjunction. (Item 1 is an example.)

1. Steve enlisted in the army [but] now he hates it.

2. You can go out Vine Street or you can take Reading Road to Paddock.

3.   The ceiling is white and the walls are blue.

4.   The phone has been ringing constantly all day, but I don't want to answer it.

5.   The television was an expensive one, so the burglar stole it.

6.   The clouds were threatening rain any minute, yet Karen still insisted on going to the park.

7.   Those two ladies are very old and they are very kind.

8.   Age cannot destroy her beauty, nor can pain kill her spirit.

9.   The moon goes around the earth and the earth goes around the sun.

10.   Jane has a lovely voice but she sings too loud.

Use the answer key to check your work. Mark the results below. Then discuss any incorrect answers with your instructor.

No. Correct: . . . .   *No. Incorrect: . . . .*

The word *and* is not automatically a sign of a compound sentence. A coordinate conjunction can be used to make compound subjects and compound verbs, for example, as well as compound sentences.

EXAMPLES

    s   s   v   v
Bob | and | Pam washed | and | waxed the car.
(This is a simple sentence with a compound subject and a compound verb.)

    s   v   s   v
Bob washed the car | and | Pam waxed it.
(This is a compound sentence.)

          s   v   v
A white cat brushed against my pants | and | left fur on them.
(This is a simple sentence with a compound verb.)

To have a compound sentence you must have a main clause with a subject and a verb on both sides of the coordinate conjunction.

● EXERCISE 82

Underline each subject and each verb in the following sentences. Put boxes around *all* the coordinate conjunctions. If the coordinate conjunction joins two main clauses, mark the sentence *C* for compound sentence. (Item 1 is an example.)

1. The <u>kitten</u> <u>pounced</u> on the lady $\boxed{and}$ the <u>lady</u> <u>giggled</u> $\boxed{and}$ <u>wriggled</u>. *C*

2. Jan and Dean sang songs about surfing.

3. The operator of the press pulled the lever and started the machine rolling.

4. You can bring me a clean shirt and a jacket, but you can forget the tie.

5. At last the snow stopped, for the sky had cleared, so we packed the car and took off.

Use the answer key to check your work. Mark the results below. Then discuss any incorrect answers with your instructor.

No. Correct: . . . . . .   *No. Incorrect:* . . . .

● EXERCISE 83

Write two simple sentences of your own. Then combine them into a compound sentence by using a *coordinate conjunction*.

EXAMPLE

Simple: Mary's children are home for the holidays.
Simple: Mary is bursting with joy.
Compound: Mary's children are home for the holidays, *so* Mary is bursting with joy.

1. *Simple:* . . . .

. . . .

Simple: ....

....

Compound: ....

....

....

2. *Simple:* ....

....

Simple: ....

....

Compound: ....

....

....

3. *Simple:* ....

....

Simple: ....

....

Compound: ....

....

....

4. *Simple:* ....

....

Simple: . . . .

. . . .

Compound: . . . .

. . . .

. . . .

5. *Simple:* . . . .

. . . .

Simple: . . . .

. . . .

Compound: . . . .

. . . .

. . . .

Show your work to your instructor. Mark your score below.

No. Correct: . . . .   *No. Incorrect:* . . . .

2. Use a Semicolon

A semicolon (;) joins two main clauses to make a compound sentence.

> *EXAMPLES*
>
> The morning paper predicted rain $\boxed{;}$ the evening paper predicted fair weather.
>
> I feel good remembering Bill $\boxed{;}$ his kind ways cheer me even in memory.

In a compound sentence with very short main clauses, a comma may be used instead of a semicolon.

EXAMPLE

S   V   S   V   S   V
I came⬚I saw⬚I conquered.

● EXERCISE 84

In the following compound sentences, underline the subject and the verb in each main clause. Put a box around the semicolon. (Item 1 is an example.)

1. The man on the right works at Procter and Gamble ⬚ the man on the left works at Formica.

2. Tomorrow we will think about our problems; tonight we will relax in our own special way.

3. John loves honey; he has honey every day.

4. Acrophobia is the fear of heights; hydrophobia is the fear of water.

5. The restaurant lowered its prices; as a result, its business increased greatly.

Use the answer key to check your work. Mark the results below. Then discuss any incorrect answers with your instructor.

No. Correct: . . . .   *No. Incorrect:* . . . .

● EXERCISE 85

Write two simple sentences of your own. Then combine them into a compound sentence by using a semicolon.

1. *Simple:*   . . . .

                   . . . .

   Simple: . . . .

                   . . . .

Compound: . . . .

. . . .

. . . .

2. *Simple:*   . . . .

. . . .

Simple: . . . .

. . . .

Compound: . . . .

. . . .

. . . .

3. *Simple:*   . . . .

. . . .

Simple: . . . .

. . . .

Compound: . . . .

. . . .

. . . .

Show your work to your instructor. Mark your score below.

No. Correct: . . . .   *No. Incorrect:* . . . .

A Special Case

A commonly used compound sentence construction with the words
however, therefore, furthermore, and *nevertheless* uses a semicolon
before these words and a comma after them.

> *EXAMPLES*
>
> s   v   s   v   v
> I love to go to the movies; however, I haven't had the time
>   lately.
>
>   s   v   s
> The students in this class are very capable; furthermore, they
>   v
>   always do their assignments on time.

● EXERCISE 86

In the following compound sentences, underline the subject and the verb in
each main clause. Put a box around the semicolon, the joining word, and the
comma. (Item 1 is an example.)

1. The conductor gave the downbeat; nevertheless, no sound came from the
    orchestra.

2. The chairman of the committee was calling for order; however, the mem-
    bers ignored him.

3. The cost of living continues to rise; therefore, everyone needs a raise in
    wages.

4. I take orders from nobody; furthermore, you can blow it out your ear.

5. Freedom to be oneself presupposes financial security; however, the
    majority of Americans are slaves to the marketplace.

Use the answer key to check your work. Mark the results below. Then discuss
any incorrect answers with your instructor.

No. Correct: . . . .   *No. Incorrect:* . . . .

● EXERCISE 87

Write two simple sentences of your own. Then combine them into a compound sentence using either *however*, *therefore*, *furthermore*, or *nevertheless*, whichever one makes sense. Also use the proper punctuation.

1. *Simple:* . . . .

   . . . .

   Simple: . . . .

   . . . .

   Compound: . . . .

   . . . .

   . . . .

2. *Simple:* . . . .

   . . . .

   Simple: . . . .

   . . . .

   Compound: . . . .

   . . . .

   . . . .

Show your work to your instructor. Mark your score below.

No. Correct: . . . .   *No. Incorrect:* . . . .

● EXERCISE 88

Mark each of the following groups of words *C* if it is a compound sentence or *S* if it is a simple sentence. Underline each subject and verb.

1. Their baseball team lost every game this year.

2. The microwave oven cooks food very fast but it also may be dangerous to use.

3. Peggy liked the people and the physical beauty of the Mexican country-side.

4. The football coach seems to hate people and he always acts angry.

5. John and Cindy met in the back of a blue pickup truck at five o'clock.

6. They danced and sang under the clear sky with a great feeling feeling of joy until dinnertime, and then they ate and drank for hours.

7. Tom dreamed of inviting a frog to breakfast and he woke up feeling absurd.

Use the answer key to check your work. Mark the results below. Then discuss any incorrect answers with your instructor.

No. Correct: . . . .   *No. Incorrect:* . . . .

Review: Main Clauses and Subordinate Clauses

To understand complex sentences, you need to understand clauses. A *clause* is a group of words that has a subject and a verb that go together. There are two types of clauses:

1. Main clauses.
2. Subordinate clauses.

A *main clause* can stand by itself as a sentence.

EXAMPLE

        s   v
The cat scratched the legs of the table.

A *subordinate clause* cannot stand alone as a sentence. A subordinate clause is only a fragment of a sentence; it must be attached to a main clause to make a correct sentence. You can recognize a subordinate clause by the fact that it begins with a subordinate conjunction.

EXAMPLE

       s   v

because she was restless

Another way to recognize a subordinate clause is to think of it as a main clause with a subordinate conjunction in front of it.

EXAMPLE

I was washing the dishes.   (main clause)

when I was washing the dishes   (subordinate clause)

● EXERCISE 89

Underline the subject and the verb in each of the following clauses. Put two lines under the subordinate conjunction at the beginning of each subordinate clause. Capitalize the first word and put a period at the end of each main clause.

1. since the cup is dirty

2. the cup is dirty

3. he has a crush on Claire

4. if he breaks the brick with one blow

5. my neighbor took the bus to work every day last week

6. although he owns a car

7. which she found

8. the cook likes people with fat faces

Use the answer key to check your work. Mark the results below. Then discuss any incorrect answers with your instructor.

No. Correct: . . . .   *No. Incorrect:* . . . .

COMPLEX SENTENCES

A complex sentence has at least one main clause and at least one subordinate clause. It may have more than one of either type of clause.

REMINDER: A subordinate clause is like a main clause except that it begins with a subordinate conjunction.

EXAMPLES

When the bell rings, the exam will begin.

(This complex sentence has one main clause and one subordinate clause.)

The exam questions will be passed out and the exam will begin when the bell rings.

(This complex sentence has two main clauses and one subordinate clause.)

When the bell rings, the exam that you have been waiting for will begin.

(This complex sentence has one main clause and two subordinate clauses.)

A complex sentence is the only sentence type that uses subordinate clauses.

Subordinate Clauses

Subordinate clauses function in two ways:

1. As modifiers.
2. As subjects or objects.

The more important and common function is as modifiers.

Subordinate Clauses as Modifiers

As modifiers, subordinate clauses function as:

    1. Modifiers of verbs.

    2. Modifiers of subjects or objects.

Subordinate Clause as a Modifier of a Verb

A subordinate clause that modifies a verb always begins with a subordinate conjunction such as these:

after	though	as if
although	unless	as long as
as	until	even though
because	when	in order that
before	whenever	so that
if	where	
since	wherever	
than	while	

(There are others, but these are the most common ones.)

Word Order

A subordinate clause that modifies a verb can be placed either *before* or *after* the main clause.

Punctuation

If the subordinate clause comes first, there usually is a comma *between* it and the main clause. (If the subordinate clause comes after the main clause, the comma between them is optional.)

    EXAMPLES

    When the bell rings⎡,⎤the exam will begin.
    The exam will begin when the bell rings.

    Although the shoes were expensive⎡,⎤Wendy bought them.
    Wendy bought the shoes⎡,⎤although they were expensive.

● EXERCISE 90

In the following complex sentences, underline the whole subordinate clause and put a box around the *subordinate conjunction*. Mark *s* above the subject and *v* above the verb in each main clause and each subordinate clause. (Item 1 is an example.)

1. [Because] butter costs too much money, people are using more margarine.

2. The telephone rang while I was taking a shower.

3. Since you are here, you may stay for dinner.

4. The man whistled at the woman as she walked by.

5. Whenever I wash my car, it always rains.

6. Officials of the government should enforce laws against air pollution, because air pollution can harm everyone's health.

7. Carl visited the old neighborhood where he had lived as a child.

8. Even though the teacher had placed the order early, the bookstore did not have the book for his class on the shelf.

9. If the moon turned into a bird and flew away, Gail would not raise her eyes.

10. The negotiations to settle the strike will collapse unless management meets the union's demands.

Use the answer key to check your work. Mark the results below. Then discuss any incorrect answers with your instructor.

No. Correct: . . . .   *No. Incorrect:* . . . .

● EXERCISE 91

Write five complex sentences of your own using a subordinate conjunction from the list on p. 115 to begin the subordinate clause. Underline the whole subordinate clause and put a box around the *subordinate conjunction.*

1. ....

   ....

   ....

2. ....

   ....

   ....

3. ....

   ....

   ....

4. ....

   ....

   ....

5. ....

   ....

   ....

Show your work to your instructor. Mark your score below.

No. Correct: . . . .   *No. Incorrect:* . . . .

Subordinate Clauses as Modifiers of Subjects or Objects

A subordinate clause that modifies a subject or an object begins with one of these words:

```
that            who             which
                whose
```

Subordinate Clause as a Modifier of a Subject

Word Order

The subordinate clause comes right after the word it modifies.

Punctuation

Commas can be used at the beginning and end of subordinate clauses that modify subjects. (If you use commas, be sure to use them at both the begin ning and the end.)

EXAMPLES

$$\overset{s}{\text{London}}[,]\underline{\text{which is the capital of England}}[,]\overset{v}{\text{is a major financial}}$$
center.

$$\text{The people }\overset{s}{\underline{\text{who live next door}}}\overset{v}{\text{come from Florida.}}$$

$$\text{The }\overset{s}{\text{ballplayer}}[,]\underline{\text{whose book sold a million copies}}[,]\overset{v}{\text{hired a tax}}$$
lawyer.

EXCEPTION: *Never* put commas at the beginning and the end of a subordinate clause starting with *that*.

$$\text{The }\overset{s}{\text{money}}\underline{\text{that you found on the table}}\overset{v}{\text{belongs to me.}}$$

NOTE: A subordinate clause that modifies the subject comes *between* the subject and the verb of the main clause.

● EXERCISE 92

Underline the whole subordinate clause in the following complex sentences. Mark *s* above the subject and *v* above the verb *of the main clause.* (Item 1 is an example.)

        S   V

1. John Glenn, <u>who was an astronaut,</u> is now a United States Senator.

2. The doctor, whose name is Jenkins, charges twenty dollars.

3. The bucket, which has a hole in it, dribbled a trail of water across the floor.

4. The music that Christine's parents like the best comes from the thirties.

5. Those girls, who we met at a party Saturday night, refuse to talk to us.

6. An air conditioner that uses a lot of electricity can run up the utility bill sky high.

7. The boys who are leaning on the car are my son and a friend of his.

Use the answer key to check your work. Mark the results below. Then discuss any incorrect answers with your instructor.

No. Correct: . . . .   *No. Incorrect:* . . . .

● EXERCISE 93

Write four complex sentences of your own with a subordinate clause modifying the subject of the main clause. Underline the whole subordinate clause.

1.   . . . .

    . . . .

    . . . .

2.   . . . .

. . . .

. . . .

3.   . . . .

. . . .

. . . .

4.   . . . .

. . . .

. . . .

Show your work to your instructor. Mark your score below.

No. Correct: . . . .   *No. Incorrect:* . . . .

Subordinate Clause as a Modifier of an Object

Word Order

Again the subordinate clause comes *right after* the word it modifies.

> *EXAMPLES*
>
>   o
> The baby has broken the toy <u>that his grandmother gave him.</u>
>
>   o
> The dealer shook the hand of the man <u>who bought the used car.</u>
>
>   o
> First prize went to the man <u>whose specialty was cherry pie.</u>
>
>   o
> He showed me the picture, <u>which he always carries in his wallet,</u>
> of his first love.

NOTE: As in the last example above, sometimes part of the main clause comes *after* this kind of subordinate clause.

● EXERCISE 94
_____

Underline the whole subordinate clause in the following complex sentences.

1. Carl gave Deena a diamond ring, which she has always wanted.

2. Every person seeks those things that make him happy.

3. Mary knows a doctor who makes house calls.

4. The sheriff is looking for the man whose brother escaped from the work-house.

5. Carefully Hal carried the groceries, which Esther had purchased, into the house.

Use the answer key to check your work. Mark the results below. Then discuss any incorrect answers with your instructor.

No. Correct: . . . .   *No. Incorrect:* . . . .
_____

● EXERCISE 95
_____

Write four complex sentences of your own with a subordinate clause modifying an object. Underline the whole subordinate clause.

1.   . . . .

     . . . .

     . . . .

2.   . . . .

     . . . .

     . . . .

3.   . . . .

     . . . .

     . . . .

4.   . . . .

. . . .

. . . .

Show your work to your instructor. Mark your score below.

No. Correct: . . . .   *No. Incorrect:* . . . .

● EXERCISE 96

Underline the whole subordinate clause in the following complex sentences.
Mark *s* above the subject and *v* above the verb *of the main clause.* (Item 1 is
an example.)

1. The car that is passing by has a broken muffler.

2. The man greeted the brother that he hadn't seen for six years in a warm
    manner.

3. The telephone company finally sent him the money that they had owed
    him for seven months.

4. Tom, who never learned how to settle down, hates school.

5. David, who always has an eye for the ladies, now has his eye on Becky.

6. Unfortunately, Becky, who is more interested in studying than dating,
    avoids David.

7. The record that I told you about is on sale downtown.

8. Truthfulness is an ideal which many people find impossible to live up to.

9. The seeds that you are planting now will bear fruit later.

10. I was helped a great deal by the information that you gave me yesterday.

Use the answer key to check your work. Mark the results below. Then discuss any incorrect answers with your instructor.

No. Correct: . . . .   *No. Incorrect:* . . . .

Two simple sentences that are about the same person or thing can be made into a complex sentence by using *which, that,* or *who.* One simple sentence becomes the main clause of the complex sentence, while the other one becomes the subordinate clause. The main clause should carry the information that you think is more important.

Study the following examples carefully.

EXAMPLES

1. The car has a V-8 engine.
   The car costs more than five thousand dollars.

   The car, which has a V-8 engine, costs more than five thousand dollars.

2. The building used to stand on the corner.
   The building was torn down for urban renewal.

   The building that used to stand on the corner was torn down for urban renewal.

3. Former President Nixon is living in San Clemente.
   Former President Nixon receives a sizable pension.

   Former President Nixon, who is living in San Clemente, receives a sizable pension.

4. Little Joe found a knife.
   The knife had a broken blade.

   Little Joe found a knife which had a broken blade.

5. I am going to punish the dog.
   The dog chewed my shoe to pieces.

   I am going to punish the dog that chewed my shoe to pieces.

6. The patient rang for the nurse.
   The nurse gives him a massage.

   The patient rang for the nurse who gives him a massage.

● EXERCISE 97

Write two simple sentences about each of the following persons or things. Then combine the sentences into a complex sentence using *which*, *that*, or *who*.

1. the picture   *Simple:*   . . . .

. . . .

Simple: . . . .

. . . .

Complex: . . . .

. . . .

. . . .

2. John Kennedy   *Simple:*   . . . .

. . . .

Simple: . . . .

. . . .

Complex: . . . .

. . . .

. . . .

3. the bag   *Simple:*   . . . .

. . . .

Simple: . . . .

. . . .

Complex: ....

....

....

4. Martin Luther King *Simple:* ....

....

Simple: ....

....

Complex: ....

....

....

5. the bed *Simple:* ....

....

Simple: ....

....

Complex: ....

....

....

Show your work to your instructor. Mark your score below.

No. Correct: ....   *No. Incorrect:* ....

Subordinate Clauses as Subjects or Objects

A subordinate clause that functions as a subject or an object begins
with one of the following words:

that	whoever
what	whatever

NOTE: *Never* use a comma to separate a subject or an object from the
verb it goes with. This rule holds true even when the subject or the
object is a whole subordinate clause.

EXAMPLES

What you want is impossible.
    (The whole clause *What you want* is the subject of the verb
    is.)

Whoever leaves last should lock the door.
    (The whole clause is the subject of the verb *should lock.*)

Whatever you do is all right with me.
    (The whole clause is the subject of the verb *is.*)

She said that she was ready.
    (The whole clause is the object of the verb *said.*)

I know what I want to do.
    (The whole clause is the object of the verb *know.*)

● EXERCISE 98

Underline the whole subordinate clause in the following complex sentences.
If it is a subject, mark *s* above it; if it is an object, mark *o* above it. (Item 1 is
an example.)

                    O
1. John hoped that he could find a job.

        S
2. What we have here is a failure to communicate.

3. You can do whatever you want.

4. At first the operator said that the phone was out of order.

5. Whoever is bitten by mosquitoes will spend the whole night scratching.

6. Some people cannot understand what other people are saying.

7. Whatever Gary tries always turns out a success.

8. Because of her fearful nature, Janice often expected that disaster was waiting for her just around the corner.

9. Give the package to whoever calls for it.

Use the answer key to check your work. Mark the results below. Then discuss any incorrect answers with your instructor.

No. Correct: . . . .   *No. Incorrect:* . . . .

● EXERCISE 99

Write four complex sentences of your own where the subordinate clause functions either as a subject or an object. Underline the whole subordinate clause.

1.   . . . .

. . . .

. . . .

2.   . . . .

. . . .

. . . .

3.   . . . .

. . . .

. . . .

4. . . . .

. . . .

. . . .

Show your work to your instructor. Mark your score below.

No. Correct: . . . .   *No. Incorrect:* . . . .

The word *that* sometimes may be dropped at the beginning of a subordinate clause.

> *EXAMPLES*
>
> I know we can make it.
> I know that we can make it.
>
> He could not find the record he wanted.
> He could not find the record that he wanted.
>
> All we have to do is try.
> All that we have to do is try.

● EXERCISE 100

In the following sentences, add *that* where it has been left out. (The first item is an example.)

1. Albert said ⌃*that* he was too busy to party.

2. Doris lost the sweater her aunt gave her for her birthday.

3. The farmers hoped next year would be better.

4. The man Ann saw standing behind the counter ignored her.

5. Here are the flowers Warren bought for the girl he is taking out.

Use the answer key to check your work. Mark the results below. Then discuss any incorrect answers with your instructor.

No. Correct: . . . .   *No. Incorrect:* . . . .

Long Complex Sentences

To be a complex sentence, a sentence must have one main clause and one subordinate clause. But it can have more of each type of clause. Study the following examples carefully.

EXAMPLES

(The subordinate clauses are underlined.)

When Susan finds something that offers her a challenge, she works harder.

My mother is always lecturing me; she says that I should be respectful to everyone.

As we searched through the deserted mansion, we noticed that in the library one of the shelves which were crammed full of books had collapsed under the weight. (Notice that here one subordinate clause contains another subordinate clause, which is double underlined.)

Because much of what they do is done in secret, politicians can use the control that they have over people's lives for either good or evil purposes.

● EXERCISE 101

Underline every subordinate clause in the following complex sentences. Put a box around the subordinate conjunction at the beginning of the subordinate clauses. (Look for subordinate conjunctions and for subjects and verbs if you are not sure where one clause ends and another clause begins.) (Item 1 is an example.)

1. If he does not lie about the fact that his father was connected with organized crime, Senator Hollister will probably win reelection.

2. When we were in the Rocky Mountains, we went camping with Paul, who taught us how to hunt and fish.

3. The man in a reddish-brown hat walked with determination across the room; then he slugged the man who had insulted him.

4. Even though Sue is allergic to chicken soup, her grandmother makes her eat it all the time because she believes that chicken soup can make everybody healthy.

5. While he was in town, the owner of the Pirates saw his team play and he liked what he saw.

Use the answer key to check your work. Mark the results below. Then discuss any incorrect answers with your instructor.

No. Correct: . . . .   *No. Incorrect:* . . . .

● EXERCISE 102

Write four long complex sentences of your own. (Each sentence should have at least three clauses.) Underline the subordinate clauses.

1.   . . . .

 . . . .

 . . . .

2.   . . . .

 . . . .

 . . . .

3.   . . . .

 . . . .

 . . . .

4.   . . . .

 . . . .

 . . . .

Show your work to your instructor. Mark your score below.

No. Correct: . . . .   *No. Incorrect:* . . . .

Review: The Three Sentence Types

There are three types of grammatically correct sentences. They are defined according to how many and what types of clauses they contain.

A *simple sentence* has one main clause.

A *compound sentence* has two or more main clauses.

A *complex sentence* has at least one main clause and at least one subordinate clause.

● EXERCISE 103: REVIEW

Underline each subject and each verb in all the clauses in the following sentences. Mark each sentence either *S* for simple sentence, *C* for compound sentence or *CX* for complex sentence.

1. Often Edgar wasted his energy shoveling snow.

2. The hunter had bagged two young lions, when suddenly the mother lion attacked him.

3. Lenny and Sue have been wanting to return home for a visit for a long time and at last they will make the trip next week.

4. Annie, softening to Joe's sweet talk, yielded to the warmth of his loving embrace.

5. Some prisons use mind-altering drugs on prisoners; they control or punish the prisoners with the drugs.

6. To get to Atlanta quickly, you should take Interstate 75.

7. Because the brakes failed, the car smashed into a telephone pole.

8. Puddles of water covered the tennis courts, so the tennis players prayed for sun.

9. Nobody could think about anything except the vacation which was about to begin.

10. The runner ran around third base and scored the winning run.

Use the answer key to check your work. Mark the results below. Then discuss any incorrect answers with your instructor.

No. Correct: . . . .   *No. Incorrect:* . . . .

● EXERCISE 104

Write three simple sentences of your own.

1.   . . . .

. . . .

2.   . . . .

. . . .

3.   . . . .

. . . .

Write three compound sentences of your own.

1.   . . . .

. . . .

. . . .

2.   . . . .

. . . .

. . . .

3. . . . .

. . . .

. . . .

Write three complex sentences of your own.

1. . . . .

. . . .

. . . .

2. . . . .

. . . .

. . . .

3. . . . .

. . . .

. . . .

Show your work to your instructor. Mark your score below.

No. Correct: . . . .   *No. Incorrect:* . . . .

● EXERCISE 105

Write a paragraph about one of the following topics. Use a variety of sentences — simple, compound, and complex — to show what you have learned from this section.

Topics:

Your ideal job.

Your ideal mate.

Your most important learning experience in the past few months.

Your paragraph should have:

1.   A sentence at the beginning giving your controlling idea.
2.   At least six sentences that develop your idea.
3.   A concluding sentence.

. . . .

. . . .

. . . .

. . . .

. . . .

. . . .

. . . .

. . . .

. . . .

. . . .

. . . .

. . . .

. . . .

. . . .

. . . .

. . . .

Show your paragraph to your instructor.

You have now finished *Section Four*, Sentence Types. Now go
on to *Section Five*, Sentence Errors and Corrections.

SECTION FIVE

Sentence Errors and Corrections

The work you have done in this book has been directed toward helping you learn to write grammatically correct sentences in your essays or papers for classes, in job applications, and so on. Now that you have done this work, you have both the necessary knowledge and experience to write correct sentences whenever you need or want to. Just remember that there are only *three* types of grammatically correct sentences — simple, compound, and complex — and make sure that all the sentences you write fit one of these three types.

Here is a suggestion on a way to apply what you have learned about sentences to your essay writing:

1. First, write freely, concentrating on saying what you want to say. Do not worry much at this stage about whether or not your sentences are grammatically correct.

2. After you have put down on paper what you want to say, *then* check your sentences to see if they are simple, compound, or complex. If you are not sure whether a particular sentence is correct, take it out of the essay, write it down separately, and look at it. If it is not a simple, compound, or complex sen-

tence, then it is incorrect. Rewrite it, making it one of the three types.

Still, sentences are complicated matters, and errors are often made. This section goes into detail about the most commonly made errors and gives you practice in methods of correcting them.

Commonly made errors are related to each type of sentence:

1. Phrase fragments are errors related to simple sentences.
2. Comma-splices and fused sentences are errors related to compound sentences.
3. Subordinate clause fragments are errors related to complex sentences.

To correct these errors, you need these skills:

1. The skill to recognize subjects and verbs that go together.
2. The skill to distinguish between phrases and main clauses and subordinate clauses.

Review: Clauses and Phrases

A *phrase* is any group of words that does *not* have both a subject and a verb.

Every clause has a subject and a verb. This includes both main clauses and subordinate clauses.

A *main clause* makes a sentence.

A *subordinate clause* begins with a *subordinate conjunction* and therefore cannot be a sentence by itself.

● EXERCISE 106: REVIEW

Underline the subject and the verb in the following groups of words. If there is no subject and verb, write *phrase* next to the group of words. Put two lines under the subordinate conjunction at the beginning of *every* subordinate clause. Capitalize the first word and put a period at the end of each main clause.

EXAMPLES

1. jumping over the puddle *phrase*

2. when the sun appears after the clouds break

3. ^{T}the <u>water</u> <u>went</u> down ⊙

4. the lady singing the lead role   *phrase*

1. since I fell for you

2. below the dressing table

3. dropped on his head

4. the patient held on either side by attendants in white

5. he left

6. because of the earthquake

7. because he is looking for a better way

8. the man playing second base for the home team

9. the dog chased it

10. running up and down the steps as fast as he could run

11. the dancer that was attracting all the attention

12. although the dresses that the girls planned to wear at the wedding were ready on time

13. the druggist looked under the counter

14. due to the reflection of the lights in the mirror

15. an idea whose time has come

Show your work to your instructor. Mark your score below.

No. Correct: . . . .   *No. Incorrect:* . . . .

If you had errors in more than three of the items in this exercise, turn to p. 84 in *Section Three*, <u>Sentence Elements</u> and review the material on recognizing verbs and on <u>distinguishing between phrases and main clauses and subordinate clauses.</u>

RECOGNIZING SUBJECTS AND VERBS: A SPECIAL CASE

Sometimes a group of words may contain what looks like a subject and a verb, but what looks like the verb is really a participle, and the participle is modifying the word that looks like the subject.

Study the differences between the following examples carefully.

EXAMPLES

1.   the tree falling on the car   (phrase)

s   v
The tree is falling on the car.   (clause)

s   v
The tree falling on the car broke the windshield.   (clause)

2.   the ball dropped by the catcher   (phrase)

s   v
The ball was dropped by the catcher.   (clause)

s   v
The ball dropped by the catcher allowed a runner to score.
(clause)

3.   the money found on the thief   (phrase)

s   v
The money was found on the thief.   (clause)

s   v
The money found on the thief belonged to me.   (clause)

As these examples show, there are two ways to give the word that looks like a subject a verb for it to go with:

1.   Add helping verbs *in front of* the participle.
2.   Add a verb (and any other words necessary to make a meaningful statement) *after* the participial phrase.

● EXERCISE 107

Change the following phrases into *main clauses*. Change each phrase in the two ways just explained.

1.   the man running down the street

(a) ....

....

(b) ....

....

2. the uniforms provided by the company

(a) ....

....

(b) ....

....

3. Bob sitting quietly in his chair

(a) ....

....

(b) ....

....

4. the letter written to the president

(a) ....

....

(b) ....

....

5. Ann taking the bus to work

(a) ....

....

(b) ....

....

Show your work to your instructor. Mark your score below.

No. Correct: ....   *No. Incorrect:* ....

DISTINGUISHING BETWEEN MAIN CLAUSES AND SUBORDINATE CLAUSES: SOME SPECIAL CASES

A main clause can stand by itself as a sentence. A subordinate clause is only a fragment of a sentence. But these facts do not mean that a main clause is necessarily longer than a subordinate clause. In fact, a subordinate clause has an extra element that a main clause does not have; this extra element is the subordinate conjunction.

A main clause may have only two words and still stand by itself as a sentence. A subordinate clause may have twenty words and still be only a fragment of a sentence.

EXAMPLES

s   v
She wept.   (main clause)

                           s
when the gentle breeze from the shimmering lake lightly
      v
brushed against her warm cheeks and soft hair with soothing
caresses   (subordinate clause)

It is possible to have a string of subordinate clauses in which one subordinate clause modifies an element in another subordinate clause.

EXAMPLE

            s   v   s   v   v   s
because Jack dropped the hammer that he was holding when he
      v
heard the sound of cars crashing

This example is not a sentence, because there is no main clause.

One type of subordinate clause is a modifier of a subject. But for a word to really be a subject it must have a verb to go with. There is no main clause unless there is a verb *after* this type of subordinate clause

EXAMPLE

         S   V

the man who saved the child from drowning in the river

The word *man* could be a subject, but it has no verb to go with, so there is no main clause. Add a verb and then there is a complete sentence.

EXAMPLE

(The main clause is underlined.)

        S   S   V

The man who saved the child from drowning in the river

      V

received a reward.

NOTE: The following is also a correct sentence:

     S V

He is the man who saved the child from drowning in the river.

The same problem can happen with a word that is not a subject but an object.

EXAMPLE

                       op   S   V

in the pocket of the coat that my sister got for her birthday

This is not a sentence because there is no main clause. Add the main clause and then you have a complete sentence.

EXAMPLE

        S   V   S   V

The price tag was in the pocket of the coat that my sister got for her birthday.

REMEMBER: For a sentence to be grammatically correct, it must have a *main clause*.

● EXERCISE 108

In the following groups of words, underline the subordinate conjunction at the beginning of *every* subordinate clause. Capitalize the first word and put a period at the end of each *main clause.*

1. he left

2. though the free concert in the park was attended by a crowd of over twenty thousand happy people

3. since Art paid for the food that everybody ate before Art even arrived

4. a girl who put her trust in the government

5. the man tried to find it

6. at the start of the race which lasted all day

7. if happiness is just an illusion that everybody holds onto although it will never come true

8. his sister was satisfied

9. because she tried

10. the pilot that the stewardess saw in the lobby

Use the answer key to check your work. Mark the results below. Then discuss any incorrect answers with your instructor.

No. Correct: . . . .   *No. Incorrect:* . . . .

● EXERCISE 109

Make the following groups of words complete sentences. Be sure that each of your sentences has a *main clause* along with the subordinate clause or clauses.

1. her friend who works for the same boss

. . . .

. . . .

. . . .

2. although the stores were not open where we usually shop

. . . .

. . . .

. . . .

3. in the new house that the Taylors bought

. . . .

. . . .

. . . .

4. because I left the water running when I answered the phone that kept
    ringing and ringing

. . . .

. . . .

. . . .

5. the girl who sneaked into the pantry where all the food was kept

. . . .

. . . .

. . . .

6. for example, when the old man sees the light in the window of the house
    where he lived as a child

. . . .

. . . .

. . . .

7. but only to find out that his wife had faked the heart attack in order to get rid of him

. . . .

. . . .

. . . .

Show your work to your instructor. Mark your score below.

No. Correct: . . . .   *No. Incorrect:* . . . .

PHRASE FRAGMENTS

A phrase is only a *part* of a correct sentence. A single phrase punctuated as a sentence is a sentence error called a *fragment*.

EXAMPLES

In the first and only real democracy.
Sending the right people the wrong message.

A string of phrases punctuated as a sentence is also a fragment.

EXAMPLES

At the first of the month.
Playing games with serious matters.
Opened by a woman in a black nightgown.
To go to Chicago by way of Indianapolis.

A group of words beginning with a word that could be a subject but that is followed only by a string of phrases is also a sentence fragment.

EXAMPLES

A boy born on a farm in central Ohio.
The painter carrying the buckets and brushes through the door.

Some phrase fragments are very complicated.

EXAMPLES

Being run down from lack of sleep and failing to eat regularly.

John, being angry at his boss for making him work overtime
without pay, besides paying a lousy salary to begin with.

All of these examples are phrase fragment errors. None of them is a
correct sentence.

Correcting Phrase Fragments

To correct a phrase fragment error, add whatever is needed to make a
main clause. Make sure that the phrase (or phrases) is part of a *main
clause* with a *subject* and a *verb*.

EXAMPLES

Error: After the first of the month.

Correction: After the first of the month, I never have any
money.

Error: Playing games with serious matters.
Correction: Ken is playing games with serious matters.

or

Playing games with serious matters, Ken broke
Judy's heart.

or

Playing games with serious matters can break someone's heart.
(All three are correct sentences.)

Error: A boy born on a farm in central Ohio.
Correction: A boy born on a farm in central Ohio has it rough
in a big city like New York.

or

Neil Armstrong was a boy born on a farm in central
Ohio.

Error: Being run down from lack of sleep and failing to eat
regularly.
Correction: Being run down from lack of sleep and failing to eat
regularly, Joseph often fell asleep at his desk.

Error: John, being angry at his boss for making him work overtime without pay, besides paying a lousy salary to
begin with.

Correction: John, being angry at his boss for making him work
overtime without pay, besides paying a lousy
salary to begin with, <u>quit his job.</u>

These corrections are only some examples of how to correct the errors.
There are lots of other words you could add to make correct sentences.
But whatever you do, there must be a main clause.

● EXERCISE 110

Correct the following phrase fragment errors. Make sure that the phrase (or
phrases) is part of a *main clause* with a *subject* and a *verb*.

1. In the second drawer from the top.

. . . .

. . . .

2. Awakened by a loud noise.

. . . .

. . . .

3. To get a head start.

. . . .

. . . .

4. The girl walking down the street.

. . . .

. . . .

5. At the opening of the new shopping center.

. . . .

. . . .

6. To go to Chicago by way of Indianapolis.

. . . .

. . . .

7. Opened by a woman in a black nightgown.

. . . .

. . . .

8. The painter carrying the buckets and brushes through the door.

. . . .

. . . .

9. Always trying his best but never really getting a fair chance to show his true ability.

. . . .

. . . .

10. Brenda, pleased with all the attention from the men in her new neighborhood and looking forward to an active social life.

. . . .

. . . .

Show your work to your instructor. Mark your score below.

No. Correct: . . . .   *No. Incorrect:* . . . .

● EXERCISE 111

Write five phrase fragment errors like the ones in the preceding exercise and then correct them.

1. *Phrase Fragment:* ....

   Correction: ....

   ....

   ....

2. *Phrase Fragment:* ....

   Correction: ....

   ....

   ....

3. *Phrase Fragment:* ....

   Correction: ....

   ....

   ....

4. *Phrase Fragment:* ....

   Correction: ....

   ....

   ....

5. *Phrase Fragment:* ....

   Correction: ....

. . . .

. . . .

Show your work to your instructor. Mark your score below.

No. Correct: . . . .   *No. Incorrect:* . . . .

● EXERCISE 112

Mark each of the following groups of words *S* if it is a simple sentence of *F* if it is a fragment. Underline the subjects and the verbs in the simple sentences.

1. The man came out of the kitchen towards him.

2. John, greeting his brother in a warm and friendly manner.

3. Reluctantly Glen paid John for his work.

4. Jimmy wants to join the Marines to learn a trade.

5. Being in a big hurry to get to the bank before closing time.

6. Delores, being a warm and friendly person, seems to like everyone.

7. The theater down the street with the big marquee and the huge neon sign.

8. The boys playing baseball and passing the time quite pleasantly and harmlessly.

9. Ron and his friend Ed are cleaning the yard and the pool to get things ready for the party this afternoon.

10. Their baseball team having practiced every afternoon in March and April and feeling ready for the big game coming up.

Use the answer key to check your work. Mark the results below. Then discuss any incorrect answers with your instructor.

No. Correct: . . . .   *No. Incorrect:* . . . .

● EXERCISE 113

The periods have been left out of the following paragraph. Put in a period at the end of each sentence. Capitalize the word following a period.

Sometimes the attitudes of doctors and their staffs make me really angry recently I visited an eye doctor with a friend our appointment was for ten in the morning we arrived punctually at the office the paneled walls were lined with people there were about ten or so at first gradually more and more people came in, sat down, leafed through magazines, smoked cigarettes, and exchanged ailments after a long time many people had gone in to see the doctor some of these people had come in after us I asked the nurse about the order of getting in to see the doctor the nurse spoke abruptly she claimed not to have any time to waste talking to me I felt insulted but could not do anything about it my friend had a thorn in a vein in his eye we didn't know any other eye doctors in town we had to wait we were kept waiting until three o'clock to punish us for asking a question we finally got into a consulting room just to wait another half-hour at last the doctor came in, smiled, joked, and calmly and efficiently took the thorn out of my friend's eye afterwards he offered to sell us some terrific steaks and ribs raising cattle turns out to be his hobby he seems to have forgotten the difference between people and cows

Show your work to your instructor. Mark your score below.

No. Correct: . . . .   *No. Incorrect:* . . . .

COMMA SPLICE AND FUSED SENTENCE

Comma-Splice Error

A comma-splice error is joining two main clauses with a comma instead of a *semicolon* or a *coordinate conjunction.*

> *EXAMPLE*
>
> *Comma Splice:*   The weather bureau predicted rain for today $\boxed{,}$ it hasn't rained yet.
>
> *Correction:*   The weather bureau predicted rain for today $\boxed{but}$ it hasn't rained yet.

Or: The weather bureau predicted rain for today $\boxed{;}$ it hasn't rained yet.

Or: The weather bureau predicted rain for today $\boxed{.\ \text{I}}$t hasn't rained yet.

Fused-Sentence Error

A fused-sentence error is placing two or more main clauses next to each other without any punctuation or any coordinate conjunction.

EXAMPLE

Fused Sentence: Aaron got a part-time job in a supermarket $\boxed{}$ now he can go to college in the fall.

Correction: Aaron got a part-time job in a supermarket $\boxed{;}$ now he can go to college in the fall.

or

Aaron got a part-time job in a supermarket $\boxed{,\ \text{so}}$ now he can go to college in the fall.

or

Aaron got a part-time job in a supermarket $\boxed{.\ \text{Now}}$ he can go to college in the fall.

As these examples show, there are three ways to correct a comma splice or fused sentence:

1. Add a *coordinate conjunction* between the main clauses.
2. Put a *semicolon* between the main clauses.
3. Put a *period* at the end of the first main clause and start the second main clause with a *capital letter*.

● EXERCISE 114

Underline the subjects and the verbs in *both* main clauses of the following sentences. Then correct the comma splice or fused-sentence error in three of the ways just explained. (Item 1 is an example.)

1. He did his work she never paid him for it.

   (a) Add $\boxed{\text{but}}$ between work and she.

   (b) Put $\boxed{;}$ between work and she.

(c)   Put a period after work[.] and capitalize [S]h e .

2. John went to the store to buy a gallon of milk, he bought an eight-pack
   of beer instead.

   (a)   . . . .

         . . . .

   (b)   . . . .

         . . . .

   (c)   . . . .

         . . . .

3. Jeff saw Cora for the first time at a dance last month, he spoke to her
   for the first time only yesterday.

   (a)   . . . .

         . . . .

   (b)   . . . .

         . . . .

   (c)   . . . .

         . . . .

4. The truck ran over a watermelon it splattered all over the highway.

   (a)   . . . .

         . . . .

   (b)   . . . .

         . . . .

(c) ....

....

5. The pass floated into his hands, he ran down the sideline clutching the ball.

(a) ....

....

(b) ....

....

(c) ....

....

6. Jack and Chuck are twins they do everything together.

(a) ....

....

(b) ....

....

(c) ....

....

7. She likes to cook fancy French food, he likes to eat hamburgers.

(a) ....

....

(b) ....

....

(c) ....

....

8. The band played a tribute to Duke Ellington their first number was "Take the 'A' Train."

(a) ....

....

(b) ....

....

(c) ....

....

9. Frank went into the army his sister went to college.

(a) ....

....

(b) ....

....

(c) ....

....

10. He won the long jump, he was disqualified in the high jump.

(a) ....

....

(b) ....

....

(c)   . . . .

. . . .

Show your work to your instructor. Mark your score below.

No. Correct: . . . .   *No. Incorrect:* . . . .

● EXERCISE 115

Write three simple sentences. Underline each subject and each verb.

Simple Sentences

1.   . . . .

. . . .

2.   . . . .

. . . .

3.   . . . .

. . . .

Turn your simple sentences into compound sentences. Underline the subject and verb in each main clause.

Compound Sentences

1.   . . . .

. . . .

. . . .

2.   . . . .

. . . .

. . . .

3.   . . . .

. . . .

. . . .

Show your work to your instructor. Mark your score below.

No. Correct: . . . .   *No. Incorrect:* . . . .

● EXERCISE 116

Periods and semicolons have been left out of the following paragraph. Put them in where they belong. Capitalize the first word after a period.

Learning to write well is a difficult but worthwhile task the most difficult, challenging, and important part of good writing is organizing ideas this really means getting your thoughts clear and in order often the easiest kind of writing to organize is a story a story usually consists of a series of events and you usually simply tell the events one after the other you begin at the beginning and go on to the end describing something or someone is more difficult here you have to choose some principle of organization for example, an object can be described from top to bottom or the other way around a place can be described first in general and then in detail but you, the writer, make the choice writing about ideas is probably more difficult than either writing a story or writing a description you have to select or discover the main idea and you have to choose good supporting ideas and details you also have to decide on the order of presenting the ideas this kind of learning is a difficult challenge but it is worth the effort being able to organize ideas really means being able to think clearly and the ability to think clearly is a tremendous help all through life

Show your work to your instructor. Mark your score below.

No. Correct: . . . .   *No. Incorrect:* . . . .

SUBORDINATE CLAUSE FRAGMENTS

A subordinate clause is only *part* of a correct sentence. When a subordinate clause is punctuated as if it were a sentence, the result is a sentence error called a *fragment*.

EXAMPLES

Because the engine needed a tune-up.

Which Ben had from childhood.

A string of subordinate clauses punctuated as a sentence is also an error.

EXAMPLE

After the concert started and the crowd began to relax as the band began to get hot.
(This is just a fragment, because there is no main clause.)

A group of words beginning with a word that *could* be a subject but that is followed only by one or more subordinate clauses is another kind of fragment error.

EXAMPLES

The man who took a shortcut through the woods.

The washing machine which broke down so badly that the repairman told me to get a new one.

All of the above examples are subordinate clause fragment errors. None of them is a correct sentence.

Correcting Subordinate Clause Fragments

There are two ways to correct a subordinate clause fragment error:

1. Add a main clause.
2. Take away a subordinate conjunction.

1. Add a Main Clause

EXAMPLES

Error: Because the engine needed a tune-up.
Correction: <u>Rick took his car to the garage</u> because the engine needed a tune-up.

Error: Which Ben had from childhood.
Correction: The <u>dream</u> which Ben had from childhood <u>came
true yesterday</u>.

Error: The man who took a shortcut through the woods.
Correction: The man who took a shortcut through the woods
<u>disappeared for days</u>.

2. Take Away a Subordinate Conjunction

EXAMPLES

Error: <u>After</u> the concert started and the crowd began to relax
as the band began to get hot.
Correction: The concert started and the crowd began to relax
as the band began to get hot.

Error: The washing machine <u>which</u> broke down so badly that
the repairman told <u>me</u> to get a new one.
Correction: The washing machine broke down so badly that
the repairman told me to get a new one.

Both these ways of correcting the fragment error create a main clause,
which is necessary for a correct sentence.

● EXERCISE 117

Correct each of the following subordinate clause fragments in two ways.

1. Because good housing is not available to everyone.

(a) . . . .

. . . .

(b) . . . .

. . . .

2. When the clock strikes midnight.

(a) . . . .

. . . .

. . . .

(b)   . . . .

. . . .

. . . .

3.   Although I would like to go.

(a)   . . . .

. . . .

. . . .

(b)   . . . .

. . . .

. . . .

4.   Which he borrowed from his brother.

(a)   . . . .

. . . .

. . . .

(b)   . . . .

. . . .

. . . .

5.   Since the dream that everyone could live in harmony is no closer to
reality than it ever was.

(a)   . . . .

. . . .

. . . .

(b)   . . . .

. . . .

. . . .

6. As long as people keep striving for the goals that they believe in.

(a)   . . . .

. . . .

. . . .

(b)   . . . .

. . . .

. . . .

7. The cat that ate the canary.

(a)   . . . .

. . . .

. . . .

(b)   . . . .

. . . .

. . . .

8. The personnel manager who was looking for a replacement in the main office.

(a)   . . . .

. . . .

. . . .

(b) . . . .

. . . .

. . . .

9. A voice within him that told him to cut his losses and cut out.

(a) . . . .

. . . .

. . . .

(b) . . . .

. . . .

. . . .

10. Whenever the pressures get too heavy to bear because everybody is demanding something that I can't give.

(a) . . . .

. . . .

. . . .

(b) . . . .

. . . .

. . . .

Show your work to your instructor. Mark your score below.

No. Correct: . . . .   *No. Incorrect:* . . . .

● EXERCISE 118

Write five subordinate clause fragments like the ones in the preceding exercise and then correct them. (Make sure that your correction has a main clause so as to be a correct sentence.)

1. *Subordinate Clause Fragment:* ....

....

Correction: ....

....

....

2. *Subordinate Clause Fragment:* ....

....

Correction: ....

....

....

3. *Subordinate Clause Fragment:* ....

....

Correction: ....

....

....

4. *Subordinate Clause Fragment:* ....

....

Correction: ....

....

....

5. *Subordinate Clause Fragment:* ....

....

Correction: ....

....

....

Show your work to your instructor. Mark your score below.

No. Correct: ....   *No. Incorrect:* ....

Punctuation

Do *not* use a semicolon between a subordinate clause and a main clause. In most cases you can use a comma instead. (Use a semicolon only between two *main* clauses.)

EXAMPLE

Error: Although the flag was waving in the breeze; nobody sang along with the band playing the national anthem.

Correction: Although the flag was waving in the breeze, nobody sang along with the band playing the national anthem.

● EXERCISE 119

Correct the error in punctuation in the following sentences.

1. Patients either were turned away or put in beds in the halls; because all the regular hospital beds were full.

2. Since the boss has taken a two-week vacation to Vermont; her secretary has been able to catch up on the real serious business.

3. If anyone makes a sudden noise; it means instant death.

Use the answer key to check your work. Mark the results below. Then discuss any incorrect answers with your instructor.

No. Correct: . . . .   *No. Incorrect: . . . .*

● EXERCISE 120

Periods and semicolons have been left out of the following paragraph. Put them in where they belong. Capitalize the first letter of the word at the beginning of each sentence.

We live in a tremendously complex ever-changing society where survival requires a higher level of awareness, flexibility, and adaptability than ever before there is a great necessity for individual choice because society has become so complex and there is also a possibility of a great deal of freedom for example, men no longer can assume that the work they begin to do at twenty will be the same work they will be doing at forty women have an even wider range of choice than men they can marry and have children they can marry, have children, and also have a career or they can choose a single life and a career also women, like men, can no longer be certain that when they make a choice at twenty it will still be viable for them at forty society keeps changing and requiring different things from us however, in this fluctuating society, we also are freer than ever before to respond to our own desires to change our occupations and life styles unfortunately there may be negative effects on us of all these choices there may be problems of instability and identity on the other hand, positive effects are also possible or even probable the greater awareness and flexibility that society now demands of us can produce a heightened sense of life and we now have greater opportunity to develop more of our potential than any generation before us

Show your work to your instructor. Mark your score below.

No. Correct: . . . .   *No. Incorrect: . . . .*

CORRECTING ALL SENTENCE ERRORS

The way to correct *any* sentence error is to turn it into one of the three types of sentences that are the *only* grammatically correct types of sentences:

1. Simple sentences.
2. Compound sentences.
3. Complex sentences.

To make a correct sentence out of a sentence error, you need to do one, or both, of the following things:

1. Add, remove, or change words.
2. Add, remove, or change punctuation.

● EXERCISE 121

Correct the following sentence errors. Underline the subjects and verbs in your corrections.

1. Tony's wife is angry with him, she won't cook his meals.

    . . . .

    . . . .

    . . . .

2. In the bottom drawer of the desk.

    . . . .

    . . . .

    . . . .

3. Because her parents were too strict with her when she was in her teens.

    . . . .

. . . .

. . . .

4. Rain has been falling for a whole week the river is rising rapidly.

. . . .

. . . .

. . . .

5. The quiet man in the corner turned on by the movements of the dancers.

. . . .

. . . .

. . . .

6. The story takes place in the South, the main characters are tenant farmers.

. . . .

. . . .

. . . .

7. Howard quit his job he has no money to pay his bills.

. . . .

. . . .

. . . .

8. The officer writing a ticket for the illegally parked car.

. . . .

. . . .

. . . .

9. The lady that answered the phone.

. . . .

. . . .

. . . .

10. Family life in America is changing, the change may be for the better or for the worse.

. . . .

. . . .

. . . .

Show your work to your instructor. Mark your score below.

No. Correct: . . . .   *No. Incorrect:* . . . .

Always make sure that each sentence you write has at least *one main clause.*

If a sentence has more than one main clause, make sure that the clauses are connected correctly with either *subordinate conjunctions, coordinate conjunctions* and/or the proper punctuation.

● EXERCISE 122

Correct the following sentence errors. Underline the subjects and verbs in your corrections.

1. Under all the dirt that had built up over the years.

. . . .

. . . .

. . . .

2. The picture on the wall was crooked, Sally straightened it.

. . . .

. . . .

. . . .

3. Which she lost at the movies.

. . . .

. . . .

. . . .

4. Norman Mailer is a famous writer he is also a controversial figure.

. . . .

. . . .

. . . .

5. When the movers arrived with the furniture and started to bring it in without asking where it should go but just setting it down any old place.

. . . .

. . . .

. . . .

6. Marijuana may do damage to the brain cells it may also lessen the male sex drive.

. . . .

. . . .

. . . .

7. Bugs crawling around in the dark and getting into everything and maybe even crawling into your bed.

. . . .

. . . .

. . . .

8. I am clipping your wings, your flying is through.

. . . .

. . . .

. . . .

9. Thirty years ago movies could not show a couple in bed now anything goes.

. . . .

. . . .

. . . .

10. The speaker who was having the greatest effect on the audience, almost making them jump in the air with excitement.

. . . .

. . . .

. . . .

Show your work to your instructor. Mark your score below.

No. Correct: . . . .   *No. Incorrect:* . . . .

Final Review

These are the key terms and concepts about sentences:

Every *clause* (main clause or subordinate clause) has both a *subject* and a *verb*.

EXAMPLES

Main Clauses

S   V
She has red hair.

      S   V
The captain ordered the soldiers to start firing.

Subordinate Clauses

      S   V
after the rain stopped

   S   V   V
which she has always wanted

A *phrase* does *not* have both a subject and a verb, so a phrase is only a *fragment* of a sentence.

EXAMPLES

at the start
drinking gin and tonic
the lady sitting on the bench

Conjunctions (coordinate conjunctions and subordinate conjunctions) join one clause to another clause.

EXAMPLES

S V   S   V
She has red hair | but | her sister has brown hair
    main clause   main clause

         S   V   S   V
| After | the rain stopped, we went on a picnic.
  subordinate clause   main clause

There are *three* types of sentences defined according to the number and types of clauses they contain.

A *simple sentence* has *one main clause.*

EXAMPLES

         s   v

The <u>customer</u> <u>phoned</u> the store.

       s   v

The <u>game</u> on television <u>ran</u> into overtime.

A *compound sentence* has *two or more main clauses*, which are most commonly joined by a *coordinate conjunction*.

EXAMPLES

     s   v   s   v

<u>The customer phoned the store</u> [and] <u>the manager answered.</u>
       main clause   main clause

     s   v   s

<u>The game on television ran into overtime,</u> [so] <u>the next program</u>
         main clause

    v

<u>started late.</u>
main clause

A *complex sentence* has at least *one main clause* and at least *one subordinate clause*. Each subordinate clause begins with a *subordinate conjunction*.

EXAMPLES

            s   v   s   v

[When] <u>the sun shines, people are happy.</u>
subordinate clause   main clause

   s   v   s v   v

<u>Darlessa bought a red sportscar,</u> [which] <u>she has always wanted.</u>
     main clause   subordinate clause

● EXERCISE 123

Write two *simple sentences* of your own.

1. . . . .

   . . . .

2. . . . .

. . . .

Write two *compound sentences* of your own.

1. . . . .

. . . .

2. . . . .

. . . .

Write two *complex sentences* of your own.

1. . . . .

. . . .

2. . . . .

. . . .

Show your work to your instructor. Mark your score below.

No. Correct: . . . .   *No. Incorrect:* . . . .

● EXERCISE 124: FINAL PARAGRAPH

Write a paragraph on a subject you care about, maybe something that annoys
you in a class or at your job or in your personal life. Suggest how things can
be improved. Write as well as you can, using all the kinds of correct sentences
you have learned.

. . . .

. . . .

. . . .

. . . .

. . . .

. . . .

. . . .

. . . .

. . . .

. . . .

. . . .

. . . .

. . . .

. . . .

. . . .

. . . .

. . . .

. . . .

. . . .

. . . .

. . . .

. . . .

. . . .

Show your paragraph to your instructor.

Answer Key

SECTION ONE Sentence Fundamentals

EXERCISE 1

1. 1	2. 2	3. 1	4. 3	5. 1
6. 2	7. 3	8. 1	9. 3	10. 2

EXERCISE 3

3. subordinate clause
4. subordinate clause
5. The woman looked carefully at her friend. main clause
6. The song rang out clear and hopeful in the night. main clause
7. subordinate clause
8. The dog bit the mail carrier in the leg. main clause
9. My sister came home from the party early last night. main clause
10. subordinate clause

EXERCISE 5

3. She answered the telephone.
4. phrase
5. The announcer read a special news bulletin.
6. phrase
7. phrase
8. The important thing is to try your best.

9. His <u>sister</u> <u>is playing</u> the trumpet in the parade.

10. phrase

EXERCISE 6

1. <u>The chairs look comfortable</u> | but | <u>they feel hard.</u>
          main clause   main clause

2. <u>Peggy dived into the pool</u> | while | <u>Rose watched her.</u>
          main clause   subordinate clause

3. <u>Mrs. Smith loaned me five dollars</u> | and | <u>I will repay her next</u>
          main clause   main clause
    <u>Friday.</u>

4. | When | <u>Leon tries his hardest,</u> <u>he is always successful.</u>
      subordinate clause   main clause

5. <u>Diane did a lot of work</u> | which | <u>no one else could have done.</u>
      main clause   subordinate clause

6. <u>John talked too quickly</u> | so | <u>Mary asked him to slow down.</u>
      main clause   main clause

EXERCISE 7

      S   V
2. <u>boy</u> <u>rode</u>

      S   V
3. <u>Dr. Peeı</u> <u>charged</u>

      S   V
4. <u>airplane</u> <u>cruised</u>

      S   V
5. <u>husband</u> <u>gave</u>

EXERCISE 9

      S   V   S   V
2. <u>Richard</u> <u>ate</u> too much | so | <u>his stomach</u> <u>felt</u> bloated.

      S   V   S   V
3. <u>She</u> <u>called</u> him once more | and | <u>he</u> <u>told</u> her not to call again.

      S   V   S   V
4. <u>They</u> <u>sold</u> the store | but | <u>they</u> <u>hung</u> on to the house.

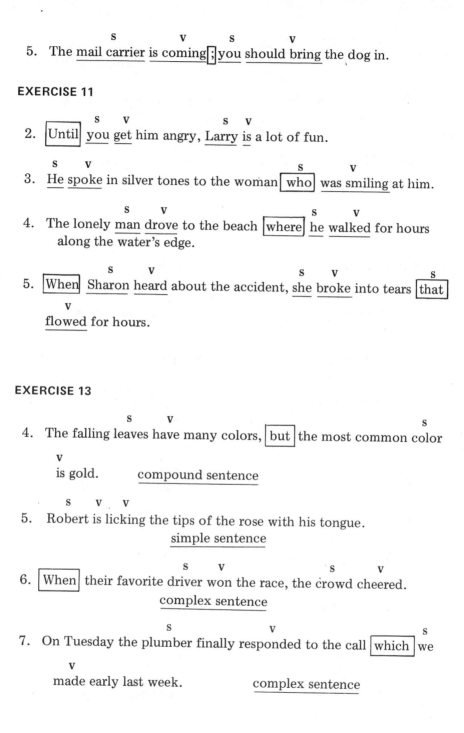

              s   v   s   v

5. The mail carrier is coming; you should bring the dog in.

EXERCISE 11

              s   v   s   v

2. Until you get him angry, Larry is a lot of fun.

    s   v   s   v

3. He spoke in silver tones to the woman who was smiling at him.

            s   v   s   v

4. The lonely man drove to the beach where he walked for hours
    along the water's edge.

               s   v   s   v   s

5. When Sharon heard about the accident, she broke into tears that
    v

    flowed for hours.

EXERCISE 13

               s   v   s

4. The falling leaves have many colors, but the most common color

    v
    is gold.   compound sentence

         s   v v

5. Robert is licking the tips of the rose with his tongue.
                 simple sentence

                 s   v   s   v

6. When their favorite driver won the race, the crowd cheered.
               complex sentence

             s   v   s

7. On Tuesday the plumber finally responded to the call which we
    v
    made early last week.   complex sentence

8.   He will unclog the stopped-up drain.   <u>simple sentence</u>

      S   V   V

9.   The clock on the wall says twelve, | but | my watch says five after twelve.   <u>compound sentence</u>

10. | Although | the odds are against us, we can succeed.   <u>complex sentence</u>

SECTION TWO Verb Recognition

EXERCISE 14

1. <u>student</u> <u>did</u>   2. <u>John</u> <u>was studying</u>

3. <u>house</u> <u>stands</u>   4. <u>water</u> <u>feels</u>

5. <u>Mother</u> <u>is sewing</u>   6. <u>apples</u> <u>look</u>

EXERCISE 15

1. v   2. nv   3. v   4. v   5. nv

6. v   7. nv   8. v   9. v   10. nv

EXERCISE 16

1. <u>laugh</u> <u>makes</u>   2. <u>sisters</u> <u>talk</u>

    people <u>laugh</u>   talk <u>was</u>

3. <u>cause</u> was   4. <u>thought</u> is

    thunderstorms <u>cause</u>   president <u>thought</u>

      s   v
5. problems <u>concern</u>

      s   v
<u>concern</u> is

EXERCISE 18

s v	s v	s v
1. We <u>caught</u>	2. I <u>buy</u>	3. <u>texture</u> is
s v	s v	s v
4. <u>book</u> looks	5. <u>dinners</u> taste	6. <u>girls</u> expected
s v	s v	
7. <u>He</u> worries	8. <u>sound</u> hurt	

EXERCISE 19

s v	s v	s v
1. <u>Betty</u> met	2. <u>Betty</u> liked	3. <u>Betty</u> had
s v	s v	s v
4. <u>She</u> told	5. <u>Bob</u> had	6. <u>children</u> hated
s v	s v	s v
7. <u>Bob</u> punished	8. <u>Betty</u> taught	9. <u>children</u> learned
s v		
10. <u>everyone</u> is		

EXERCISE 20

s v	v s	v s
1. <u>People</u> are	2. are <u>people</u>	3. is <u>book</u>
s v	s v	v s
4. <u>book</u> is	5. <u>rule</u> has	6. is <u>exception</u>
v s	v s	
7. Are <u>you</u>	8. Is <u>everyone</u>	

EXERCISE 21

2. v   helps   am helping   helped
        will help   is helping   has helped

3. nv

4. v   accepts   am accepting   accepted
        will accept   is accepting   has accepted

5. v   feels   am feeling   felt
        will feel   is feeling   has felt

6. nv

7. v   thinks   am thinking   thought
        will think   is thinking   has thought

8. nv

9. nv

10. v   believes   am believing   believed
         will believe   is believing   has believed

11. nv

12. v   sits   am sitting   sat
         will sit   is sitting   has sat

13. nv

14. v   trips   am tripping   tripped
         will trip   is tripping   has tripped

15. nv

EXERCISE 22

      s   v   s   v   s   v
1. girl ran   2. they run   3. run embarrassed

      s   v   v   s   v   s
4. job excites   5. is dog   6. Is brother

             s   v
7. vegetables taste

EXERCISE 24

1. We talked
2. We will be
3. John has gone
4. They have been dancing
5. man is looking
6. girls were
7. I will have been living
8. Simpsons have gone

EXERCISE 25

1. Kennedy is running (s)
2. Mary is going (s)
3. children didn't have (s)
4. policemen were interrogating (s)
5. Steve would drink (s)
6. Have they lost (s)
7. Is Toby running (s)
8. Does friend know (s)
9. did you have (s)
10. Has repairman called (s)

EXERCISE 26

1. I am (s)
2. I am borrowing (s)
3. Mary did (s)
4. John did do (s)
5. They have worked (s)
6. family has (s)
7. was book (s)
8. members were voting (s)

EXERCISE 28

1. I might come (s)
2. You must answer (s)

　　　　s　　　　　　　　　　　　　　s
3.　They <u>could have found</u>　　4.　goal <u>is</u>

　　　s　　　　　　　　　　　　　　s
5.　We <u>can find</u>　　　　　　　6.　<u>Does</u> Maisie <u>have</u>

　　　s　　　　　　　　　　　　　　s
7.　flowers <u>will bloom</u>　　　　8.　children <u>have been playing</u>

EXERCISE 30

2.　<u>girl</u> <u>promised</u> (to try)　　　3.　<u>You</u> <u>have</u> (to work)

4.　<u>workers</u> <u>are trying</u> (to do)　5.　<u>Mike</u> <u>wants</u> (to kiss)

6.　<u>(To win)</u> <u>is</u>　　　　　　　　7.　<u>people</u> <u>find</u> (to get)

EXERCISE 32

1.　singing　　　　2.　driving　　　　3.　sitting
4.　stabbing　　　 5.　thinking　　　 6.　running
7.　biting　　　　 8.　tripping　　　 9.　hiding
10.　seeing

EXERCISE 33

　　　s　　　v　　　　　　　　　　s　　　v
1.　<u>Smoking</u> <u>does</u>　　　　　　2.　<u>Running</u> <u>is</u>

　　　s　　　v　　　　　　　　　　s　　　　v
3.　<u>Seeing</u> <u>is making</u>　　　　4.　<u>Smiling</u> <u>encourages</u>

EXERCISE 35

1.　speaking　　　　2.　hiring　　　　3.　shutting
4.　shouting　　　　5.　clinging　　　 6.　hoping
7.　dropping　　　　8.　doing　　　　　9.　trying
10.　having

EXERCISE 36

	s	v			s	v
4.	Gregory	being succeeds		5.	barking dogs	kept

4. Gregory <u>being</u> succeeds
5. <u>barking</u> dogs kept

6. Linda <u>shutting</u> walked
7. <u>Going</u> Anna noticed

8. <u>Running</u> Jerome cut
9. <u>speeding</u> car turned

10. man sat <u>smoking</u>

EXERCISE 37

1. nv	2. v	3. nv	4. v	5. nv
6. v	7. v	8. nv	9. v	10. v

EXERCISE 38

3. <u>birds</u> <u>were chirping</u>

4. <u>birds</u> (chirping) <u>woke</u>

5. (sparkling) <u>eyes</u> <u>attracted</u>

6. <u>They</u> <u>were having</u>

7. <u>He</u> <u>has been coming</u>

8. (Turning) <u>Lili</u> <u>saw</u> (waiting)

9. <u>dancer</u> <u>was spinning</u>

EXERCISE 40

3. <u>dog</u> <u>trusted</u>

4. <u>I</u> <u>have baked</u>

5. (baked) <u>potatoes</u> <u>will be served</u>

6. <u>potatoes</u> (served) <u>cooled</u>

7. <u>Grandmother</u> <u>baked</u>

8. (exhausted) <u>child</u> <u>was sleeping</u>

9. We have exhausted

10. partygoers (exhausted) straggled

EXERCISE 42

1. known
2. left
3. gone
4. put
5. spoken
6. hidden
7. drunk
8. told
9. bought
10. brought

EXERCISE 43

4. choir sang
5. choir has sung
6. music (sung) lifts
7. candidate spoke
8. I have spoken
9. people have (spoken)
10. word (spoken) may return

EXERCISE 45

4. game was won
5. (won) race was
6. Somebody won
7. team has won
8. Cars (made) are
9. Richard made
10. Beatles have made

EXERCISE 47

	s	v
1.	museums	provide

	s	v
2.	runner	ran

	s	v
3.	Doris	opened

	s	v
4.	air	was

	s	v
5.	Annie	yielded

	s	v
6.	Unemployment	is getting

	s	v
7.	Partying	is

	s	v
8.	Sue	wants

	s	v			s	v
9.	Bert	stumbled		10.	horse	threw

	v	s	v			s	v
11.	Have	they	started		12.	hunter	killed

	s	v	v			v	s
13.	I	haven't	got		14.	are	theaters

	s	v			s	v
15.	I	enjoy		16.	pitcher	pitched

	s	v			s	v
17.	pitch	cost		18.	students	should report

	s	v			s	v
19.	I	have been following		20.	sentence	is

SECTION THREE   Sentence Elements

EXERCISE 48
1. The end of the race was marked by great confusion.
2. fragment
3. The faucet drips.
4. fragment
5. fragment
6. He laughs.
7. fragment
8. The Isle of Wight, which is in England, has an excellent climate.
9. fragment
10. They thought that they were in India.

EXERCISE 49
1. baseball
3. rifle
5. selfishness
7. Cincinnati
9. no direct object

2. no direct object
4. no direct object
6. no direct object
8. baby
10. Daniel

EXERCISE 50

      io   do   io   do
2. Sharon headache   3. me newspaper

       io   do   io   do
4. newspaper letter   5. patriotism name

EXERCISE 51

     s   v   do
1. children were eating candy

       s   v   io   do
2. Teenagers give parents time

      s   v   do
3. champion conquered challenger

     s   v   do
4. lover was climbing wall

     s   v   io   do
5. man gave pots scrubbing

EXERCISE 53

    s   s   v   v
2. Shawn |and| Ken   3. live |and| die

   v   v   do   do   io   io
4. cut |and| sewed skirt |and| blouse 5. cop |and| reporters

    s   s   v   v
6. Joe |and| I   7. cut |and| passed

   do   do
8. statue |and| sword

EXERCISE 54

   ms mdo mm mv   mv   ms   mdo
2. old busy very slowly   3. Soon whole gory

    ms   mv   mdo   ms ms   mdo mv
4. Whispering softly drowsy   5. hot tired final now

EXERCISE 55

2. with sister   3. except for carpenter

4. between them
5. behind furniture
6. because of rain
7. without friend
8. from moment
9. by process
10. in addition to giraffes

EXERCISE 56

2. In late August in spite of the heat
3. ahead of me in line about the air conditioner over our heads
4. of his two front teeth in a fight with some kids from another school
5. On Friday night on the table in the kitchen of the apartment of her closest friend

EXERCISE 58

2. flying from flower to flower
3. Excited by catnip
4. sung out of tune
5. stinking to high heaven

EXERCISE 60

2. to float gently in the breeze
3. to do in the morning
4. to drive from Chicago to New York in one day
5. To be honest

EXERCISE 62

s v 3. She is his boss.	s v 4. although she is
s v 5. I lost the watch.	s v 6. which I inherited
s v 7. as car pulled	s v 8. It hit a bump.
s v 9. The senator met his wife.	s v 10. while they were

EXERCISE 63

2. [although] everyone already knew the result

3. [because] the walls were weakened and dangerous

4. [If] the next sentence has two subordinate clauses in it

5. [Because] he had no money for the bus [where] he worked

EXERCISE 65

2. <u>lady</u> who was crying in her beer

3. <u>traveller</u> whose car ran out of gas

4. <u>shoes</u> which Lisa bought just last week

5. <u>artist</u> who gains his victims' trust

EXERCISE 67

1. <u>as you want to</u>   2. <u>than she had planned</u>

EXERCISE 68

1. s   v
    <u>sky-divers</u> <u>jump</u>

2. s   v
    <u>jump</u> <u>broke</u>

3. s   v
    <u>Richard</u> <u>jumped</u>

4. v   s
    <u>is</u> <u>book</u>

5. s   v
    <u>apartment</u> <u>depressed</u>

6. v   s
    <u>Are</u> <u>friends</u>

7. s   v
    <u>Tensions</u> <u>cause</u>

8. s   v
    <u>cause</u> <u>was</u>

9. v   s
    <u>are</u> <u>problems</u>

10. v   s
    <u>Was</u> <u>answer</u>

EXERCISE 69

1. s   v
    <u>concert</u> <u>started</u>

2. v   s
    <u>Is</u> <u>Jack</u>

3. s   v
    <u>girl</u> <u>was shopping</u>

4. s   v
    <u>(you)</u> <u>take</u>

5. v   s
    <u>is</u> <u>spot</u>

6. s   v   v
    <u>He</u> <u>should have</u> <u>pulled</u>

7. $\underset{\text{s}}{\text{I}}$ $\underset{\text{v}}{\text{surrender}}$

8. $\underset{\text{s}}{\text{surrender}}$ $\underset{\text{v}}{\text{ended}}$

9. $\underset{\text{s}}{\text{planes}}$ $\underset{\text{v}}{\text{are arriving}}$

10. $\underset{\text{s}}{\text{movements}}$ $\underset{\text{v}}{\text{are}}$

11. $\underset{\text{s}}{\text{machinists}}$ $\underset{\text{v}}{\text{have been thinking}}$

12. $\underset{\text{s}}{\text{you}}$ $\underset{\text{v}}{\text{will}}$ $\underset{\text{v}}{\text{deserve}}$

13. $\underset{\text{v}}{\text{Did}}$ $\underset{\text{s}}{\text{Edison}}$ $\underset{\text{v}}{\text{invent}}$

14. $\underset{\text{v}}{\text{will}}$ $\underset{\text{s}}{\text{you}}$ $\underset{\text{v}}{\text{put}}$

15. $\underset{\text{s}}{\text{To survive}}$ $\underset{\text{v}}{\text{is}}$

16. $\underset{\text{s}}{\text{Rhoda}}$ $\underset{\text{v}}{\text{caught}}$

17. $\underset{\text{s}}{\text{Louis}}$ $\underset{\text{v}}{\text{could}}$ $\underset{\text{v}}{\text{smile}}$

18. $\underset{\text{s}}{\text{Winning}}$ $\underset{\text{v}}{\text{requires}}$

19. $\underset{\text{s}}{\text{Earl}}$ $\underset{\text{v}}{\text{jumped}}$

20. $\underset{\text{s}}{\text{singing}}$ $\underset{\text{v}}{\text{could have broken}}$

EXERCISE 70

3. phrase

4. Gloria broke clause

5. phrase

6. phrase

7. he was feeling clause

8. phrase

9. fans shouted clause

10. phrase

EXERCISE 71

1. they come clause

2. phrase

3. phrase

4. term is clause

5. phrase

EXERCISE 73

3. The ice has melted.

4. [because] smoke burned

5. John is a nice person.

6. [although] I find

7. [that] he bought

8. The <u>desk belonged</u> to her grandfather.

9. <u>if</u> <u>group</u> <u>has</u>

10. <u>It started</u> a long time ago.

SECTION FOUR Sentence Types

EXERCISE 75

　　　　s　　v
1. <u>He</u> <u>entered</u>

　　　s　　　　v
2. <u>Deborah</u> <u>was eating</u>

　　s　　v
3. <u>dog</u> <u>smelled</u>

　　　s　　　v
4. <u>mail carrier</u> <u>spoke</u>

　　　s　　v
5. <u>worker</u> <u>saw</u>

EXERCISE 77

　　v　　　　　v
3. <u>sang</u> [and] <u>danced</u>

　　do　　　　do
4. <u>Sherry</u> [and] <u>Doug</u>

　　v　　　　v
5. <u>watched</u> [and] <u>waited</u>

　　s　　　　s　　v　　　　　v
6. <u>dog</u> [and] <u>cat</u> <u>destroyed</u> [and] <u>scattered</u>

　　s　　　　s　　do　do　　　　do
7. <u>Bill</u> [and] <u>Bob</u> <u>John</u> <u>Jack</u> [and] <u>men</u>

　　　s　　　　　s　　　do　　　　do
8. <u>bartender</u> [and] <u>customers</u> <u>chairs</u> [and] <u>table</u>

　　v　　　　　v
9. <u>loved</u> [and] <u>hated</u>

　　do　　　　do
10. <u>scorn</u> [and] <u>intent</u>

EXERCISE 79

3. <u>to the store to buy a ten-speed bicycle</u>

4. <u>for Glenn</u>

5. across the street to be broadcast next spring
6. on the desk in Barbara's office
7. Irritated by Alice's wasting time to finish washing the car right
   away
8. pressed for time across the country in just three days
9. working the bulldozer
10. filled with lilting melodies

EXERCISE 81

2. You can go [or] you can take
3. ceiling is [and] walls are
4. phone has been ringing [but] I don't want
5. television was [so] burglar stole
6. clouds were threatening [yet] Karen insisted
7. ladies are [and] they are
8. Age cannot destroy [nor] can pain kill
9. moon goes [and] earth goes
10. Jane has [but] she sings

EXERCISE 82

2. Jan [and] Dean sang
3. operator pulled [and] started
4. You can bring [and] [but] you can forget   C
5. snow stopped [for] sky had cleared [so] we packed [and] took C

EXERCISE 84

2. we will think [;] we will relax
3. John loves [;] he has
4. Acrophobia is [;] hydrophobia is
5. restaurant lowered [;] business increased

EXERCISE 86

2. chairman was calling ⎮; however,⎮ members ignored

3. cost continues ⎮; therefore,⎮everyone needs

4. I take ⎮; furthermore,⎮you can blow

5. Freedom presupposes ⎮; however,⎮majority are

EXERCISE 88

1. team lost   S

2. oven cooks it may be   C

3. Peggy liked   S

4. coach seems he acts   C

5. John Cindy met   S

6. They danced sang they ate drank   C

7. Tom dreamed he woke   C

EXERCISE 89

1. since cup is

2. The cup is dirty.

3. He has a crush on Claire.

4. if he breaks

5. My neighbor took the bus to work every day last week.

6. although he owns

7. which she found

8. The cook likes people with fat faces.

EXERCISE 90

2.   S   V   S V   V
   telephone rang ⎮while⎮ I was taking a shower

3.   S   V   S   V   V
   ⎮Since⎮you are here, you may stay

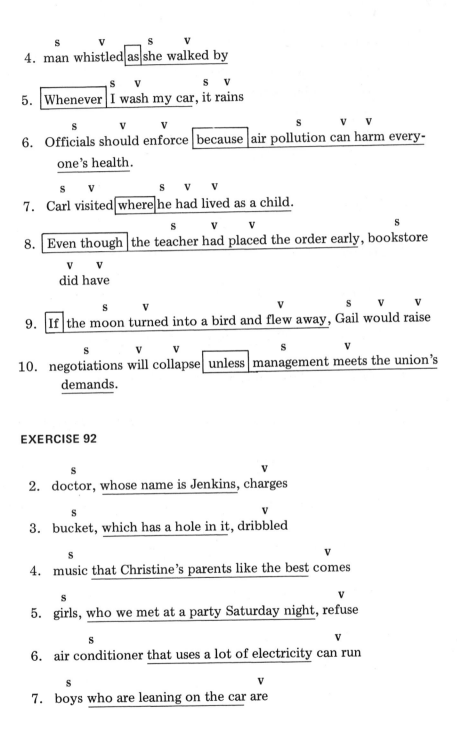

 s   v   s   v
4. man whistled|as|she walked by

           s   v   s   v
5. |Whenever|I wash my car, it rains

   s   v   v   s   v   v
6. Officials should enforce|because|air pollution can harm every-
   one's health.

   s   v   s   v   v
7. Carl visited|where|he had lived as a child.

                 s   v   v   s
8. |Even though|the teacher had placed the order early, bookstore
    v   v
   did have

        s   v   v   s   v   v
9. |If|the moon turned into a bird and flew away, Gail would raise

        s   v   v   s   v
10. negotiations will collapse|unless|management meets the union's
    demands.

EXERCISE 92

      s   v
2. doctor, whose name is Jenkins, charges

      s   v
3. bucket, which has a hole in it, dribbled

      s   v
4. music that Christine's parents like the best comes

      s   v
5. girls, who we met at a party Saturday night, refuse

         s   v
6. air conditioner that uses a lot of electricity can run

      s   v
7. boys who are leaning on the car are

EXERCISE 94

1. <u>which she has always wanted</u>
2. <u>that make him happy</u>
3. <u>who makes house calls</u>
4. <u>whose brother escaped from the workhouse</u>
5. <u>which Esther had purchased</u>

EXERCISE 96

      s   v
2. man greeted <u>that he hadn't seen for six years</u>

        s   v
3. company sent <u>that they had owed him for seven months</u>

    s   v
4. Tom, <u>who never learned how to settle down,</u> hates

    s   v
5. David, <u>who always has an eye for the ladies,</u> has

    s   v
6. Becky, <u>who is more interested in studying than dating,</u> avoids

    s   v
7. record <u>that I told you about</u> is

      s   v
8. Truthfulness is <u>which many people find impossible to live up to</u>

    s   v
9. seeds <u>that you are planting now</u> will bear

    s   v
10. I was helped <u>that you gave me yesterday</u>

EXERCISE 98

         o
3. <u>whatever you want</u>

4. <u>that the phone was out of order</u> ^o

5. <u>Whoever is bitten by mosquitoes</u> ^s

6. <u>what other people are saying</u> ^o

7. <u>Whatever Gary tries</u> ^s

8. <u>that disaster was waiting for her just around the corner</u> ^o

9. <u>whoever calls for it</u> ^o

EXERCISE 100

2. sweater │that│her
3. hoped│ that │next
4. man │that│ Ann
5. flowers │that│ Warren   girl│ that │he

EXERCISE 101

2. │When│ we were in the Rocky Mountains
   │who│ taught us how to hunt and fish

3. │who│ had insulted him

4. │Even though│ Sue is allergic to chicken soup
   │because│ she believes
   │that│ch cken soup can make everybody healthy

5. │While│ he was in town   │what│ he saw

EXERCISE 103

1. Edgar wasted   S

2. hunter had bagged lion attacked   CX

3. Lenny Sue have been wanting they will make   C

4. Annie yielded   S

5. prisons use they control punish   C

6. you should take   S

7. brakes failed car smashed   CX

8. Puddles covered players prayed   C

9. Nobody could think which was   CX

10. runner ran scored   S

SECTION FIVE   Sentence Errors and Corrections

EXERCISE 108

1. He left.

2. though

3. since that before

4. who

5. The man tried to find it.

6. which

7. if that although

8. His sister was satisfied.

9. because

10. that

EXERCISE 112

1. S man came   2. F

3. S Glen paid   4. S Jimmy wants

5. F   6. S Delores   seems

7. F   8. F

9. S Ron friend are cleaning 10. F

EXERCISE 119

1. halls because (or: halls, because)   2. Vermont, her

3. noise, it

NOTES

NOTES

NOTES

NOTES

NOTES

NOTES

NOTES